More messages
the angels

By the same author:

What the Angels Need to Tell Us Now

More messages from the angels

Preparing to receive, verifying and confirming the truth

Irene Johanson

TEMPLE LODGE

Translated from German by Pauline Wehrle

Temple Lodge Publishing
Hillside House, The Square
Forest Row, East Sussex
RH18 5ES

www.templelodge.com

Published by Temple Lodge 2002

A catalogue record for this book is available from the British Library

ISBN 1 902636 36 8

Cover by Andrew Morgan
Typeset by DP Photosetting, Aylesbury, Bucks.
Printed and bound by Cromwell Press Limited, Trowbridge, Wilts.

Contents

Publisher's Note

As with her previous work, *What the Angels Need to Tell Us Now*, this book by Irene Johanson is divided into two sections. The first part offers wise guidance on personal development and the process of receiving and judging messages from angels. This advice is based on Irene Johanson's many years' experience and work as a priest. The second part of the book contains messages and information received through a friend, Agnes, who represents a new kind of clairvoyance which does not require a dimming of individual consciousness. Rather, Agnes' ability to communicate spiritually with the angelic world has a lively character of wakefulness and clarity. In this book, she helps throw light on many urgent questions of our time.

For those who may not have read Irene Johanson's other book mentioned above — and *More Messages from the Angels* can certainly be read quite independently — the author is a priest of the Christian Community, a church founded by Friedrich Rittelmeyer with the support of Rudolf Steiner (1861–1925). The Austrian-born Steiner, known today principally for the education system he created (Steiner Waldorf education) was the founder of anthroposophy, a spiritual philosophy with a scientific basis. For the development of anthroposophy, Steiner founded the Anthroposophical Society. In contradistinction, the Christian Community was established primarily to renew religion and the Christian sacraments.

Introduction

This book is a continuation of the first volume *What the Angels Need to Tell Us Now*.* I reported in that how these angel messages came about.

Let me recapitulate briefly: In the spring of 1997 a young woman asked to speak with me. In addition to having a job she is also a housewife and mother. She lives in the country and can be said to have both feet on the ground. She told me then that for the past year she had been able to perceive angels and also the spirits of the dead or the spiritual entity of a living person. She has meditated regularly for years, and in doing so had experienced that without losing her ordinary day consciousness her spiritual sight was awakening. Either the supersensible beings approach her or she makes a connection by directing her own attention to them. As I listened to her it became clear to me that this ability was not pathalogical but something that should be taken very seriously. And I told her so. Six months later she told me that the angel of our church community wanted to speak with me. I joined her again, and without actually seeing him I experienced strongly the presence of this angel, just as sometimes in the course of an intense conversation you can experience the presence of an invisible third person. What he told me through Agnes, as the young woman was called, was something I could fully accept. This was how our collaboration began.

Agnes' request to remain incognito shows me what a selfless and realistic attitude she has to her gift. She sets

---

* Temple Lodge Publishing, 2002.

great store by not letting anything interfere with her life, either with regard to her family or professionally or socially. She also wants to deal with her gift as a communicator in freedom and undisturbed, without any pressure on her time, or pressure from the media, or the wish to profit out of it. In my opinion it is precisely this attitude which contributes to her credibility. There is also her profound truthfulness with regard to her messages and her honesty with regard to herself. It is not weakness nor cowardice but strength, when she follows her own inner principle and not the trend of the times. I would ask the reader to respect this.

Agnes once wrote in a letter: 'It is true that the hierarchies of the angels reach to great heights. We should take note of the fact that some of the angels can never enter into direct contact with human beings. Their vibrations are too high and too delicate. The angels with high vibrations would scare human beings. It would frighten them almost to death. If it is urgently necessary they will appear and say: "Do not be frightened! Fear not!"'

So it is the lowest hierarchy of angels—those who are traditionally called angeloi and who are closest to human beings—who need to make themselves known to us directly and intimately today. This is supported by a statement of Rudolf Steiner's: 'People will increasingly have to get into the habit of having an independent spiritual life. Why? Because in the fifth post-Atlantean era we are approaching a time when our perceptions—sense perceptions and supersensible perceptions—will be so constituted that the spirits of the higher hierarchies we call angels will descend further than before, and will associate much more closely with human beings. The connection between the sense world and the supersensible world will from now on become closer. People will not only receive rain from out of the clouds but will have to learn to perceive inspirations from higher regions coming to them from angels who will increasingly be living among us... In the future angels will be working together with human beings.'*

These statements have encouraged me to pass on more messages and to report on the possible ways of testing them and learning how to distinguish angel messages from those of other spirits. Another thing that encouraged me to bring out this second volume was the positive feedback from the readers of the first volume. This one is also written at the bidding of the angels. May it be received equally well and be helpful in the confusing and often difficult circumstances of our time.

---

* *Vergangenheits- und Zukunftsimpulse im sozialen Geschehen* (GA 190) lecture of 22 March 1919.

Part I

PREPARING TO RECEIVE

Distinguishing the different kinds of spirits

There is the danger today that we assume that all the beings we perceive supersensibly are good beings. A lot of people take it for granted that everything not perceptible to the bodily senses, that is, everything that is not material and earthly, is celestial and comes from heaven. Yet we should remember that even though the human soul is not material it is by no means godly! And it is similar with those invisible powers who are spiritually above the human level, ranking among the angels, and yet mislead human beings and are hostile to humankind. They are graded in hierarchies in the same way as the angels who serve God. So if not everything invisible is of a divine nature, how can we know whom we are dealing with if we are visited by a being of that kind, or receive messages from them through someone with spiritual vision?

Various requirements have to be met. First of all you have to examine yourself and your own feeling for truth. Then you have to examine the soul state of the person giving you the messages. Then, further, you have to examine the content and the way in which the person receives the messages. And finally, but not meant in the sense of the last thing to do, you have to examine the means used and the atmosphere accompanying the receiving of the message. Only when we have examined and worked on these four areas can we be certain of being able to distinguish the different kinds of spirits and thus become more and more at home with what angels need to tell us today. So before we continue reporting messages communicated through Agnes, as we had begun doing in the first volume, let us get down to acquiring a clear understanding of these four areas.

The way we are constituted

People have the habit nowadays of recognizing a thing by certain features and putting a concept to it accordingly. When we have formed the concept 'oak' for a tree, we think we know it, just as we think we know what an animal is when we know it is called a 'mole'. We often think we know a person when we know their name. We know too what a car looks like or a computer, but when it comes to technical devices we quickly reach the limits of our actual knowledge as soon as we do not know how they function. And even if we have learnt which buttons and levers to use we rapidly come to the end of our understanding if the apparatus for some reason does not work. Then we have to call in an expert. Technology can finally bring us to the point of realizing that when we know what a thing is called and recognize a few of its features we are still a long way from knowing it. To know the essence of a creature of the natural world or of a human being or of a mechanical apparatus requires much more than just knowing what they are called.

How much greater is the need for this in the case of beings who do not appear at all in material form. Yet human beings frequently respond to them in the same way. Either they deny their existence altogether, because they cannot perceive them with their senses, or they have learnt what angels look like in exactly the same way as they learn the characteristics of certain plants, human beings or physical processes, namely from the respective book on botany, anatomy or physics. We learn this method from our school days, so we do not need to be surprised if it remains deeply entrenched in us for the rest of our lives. However, if people want to become receptive to supersensible reality they must become capable of discarding this method and acquiring quite different capacities.

There are certain beings who are active in technological ware, mechanical instruments, dead apparatus. There are other beings who live in the element of illusion, unreality and confusion. And there are the kind of beings who work in the realm of life, i.e. in everything that goes through living processes, through birth—growth—transformation—death, and rebirth. Very different faculties of knowledge are required for these three different realms. The angels work in the realm of life. The element of life is not sense-perceptible nor mechanical nor static, nor does it have no relation to matter, to the sense-perceptible, to earthly activity; it is not purely accidental and fantastic, lacking in forces that bring order and form. It can not be experienced or known either through rigid concepts or through rejecting the use of concepts altogether.

What capacities do we need to do this realm justice? We can do so only by transforming all three realms of our soul life—our thinking, our feeling and our will.

Transformation of thinking

What we call thinking is generally just a moving around of our available ready-made thoughts. A person has acquired these thoughts either from school, his professional training, life experience, his world view or religion, through his own education or from examples from life. His thinking, or rather the way one thought connects with another, is determined in this way. It comes effortlessly of its own accord. It assumes the form of catch-phrases, empty words and hollow talk, etc., or is stored as information which is expressed always in the same unaltered form, without having been digested.

What has to happen to transform thinking? It must become creative. For example it is no longer enough just to be able to enumerate all the parts of a plant, but we have to recreate them in our thinking. Then our thinking does not merely link one ready-made concept to another. It slips inside the plant and follows in thinking the way the root and cotyledons come forth from the dying seed, then the stem from the shoot, how the leaves come forth from the stem, then the whole metamorphosis of the leaf right up to the formation of the bud, the blossom from the bud, stamens and pistil from the blossom, the fruit from the pollinated pistil, the seed from the fruit. In the course of this process people perform in their thinking a rhythm of expansion and contraction.

If, for some years, we bring movement into our thinking like this, with the help of plants, discovering from different plants how varied this movement of expanding and con-tracting can be, we can form in our thinking the whole being of the plant through all its stages, regardless of which sea-son the plant is passing through outside; we can create the idea of the plant in our thinking, just as Rudolf Steiner describes in his *Philosophy of Freedom*: 'Take a plant and observe it. It connects itself in our mind with a certain concept. Why should this concept belong any less to the whole plant than leaf and blossom? You say the leaves and blossoms exist quite apart from a perceiving subject, whereas the concept appears only when a human being confronts the plant. Quite so. But leaves and blossoms also appear on the plant only if there is soil in which the seed can be planted, and light and air in which the leaves and blossoms can unfold. Similarly the concept of a plant arises when someone applies his thinking consciousness to the plant.'*

Just as we can make our thinking creative through contact with nature we can also get thinking to be creative with regard to destiny, our own or others. Similar to the way there are certain ready-made concepts that can be applied to a plant: leaf, blossom, fruit, etc., there are also definite facts belonging to destiny which can be analysed: heredity, male-female, a possessive instinct, the sexual urge, desire for power, the unconscious, the conscious realm, etc. Creative thinking does not preclude that all this still belongs to a person's destiny, just as a plant's parts belong to a plant, but by means of creative thinking a person can slip into the process of destiny and arrive at the idea of this destiny, which is actually the being, the individuality of the person.

When a pupil was being discussed in a Steiner school teachers' meeting a class teacher was able to describe the posture, the walk, the form, the gestures of a pupil so vividly that the other teachers felt themselves drawn into the child so that they experienced the fact that for instance a child with a short neck, large head, stocky body build could behave in no other way than the way he did, namely to cringe psychologically but then to keep breaking out unexpectedly, often presenting problems to those around him. The act of creative thinking is necessary to have this experience. Problems become smaller and smaller for teachers to the extent that they recognize that the so-called difficulties children present belong to their destiny. Just as you can say that there is no such thing as bad weather, only unsuitable clothing, you can also say that difficult children do not exist, only rigid thinking about them.

_____

*From chapter V, 'The Act of Knowing'.

The secret about creative thinking is its paradoxical nature. We recognize what is there and how it works, and at the same time we create it anew, so that we are always alive to it. The spirit is present, whether it is the owner of the destiny, or of a natural creature or of a work of art, and these and many other such things become so real that they can be grasped as they take effect from moment to moment.

Gidon Kremer, the famous violinist, told a pupil: 'If you play a piece for the hundredth time play it as though you were improvising it that very moment!' The same thing applies to creative thinking. If you are thinking about thoughts you have thought a hundred times, be so inspired by them that the idea of a plant, of a work of art, of the individuality of a person appears spiritually at that moment in your thinking, and is experienced by you and others as though it were just being created. So thinking has to be transformed into creative will if it is to receive an idea or an individuality—that is, something supersensible—which is of course of the same element as angels.

Transformation of feeling

Our feeling usually refers to ourselves. We feel our body and whether we feel healthy or ill. We feel our moods. We feel the effect that a landscape, a piece of music, a picture, a person, a group of people has on us. Things appeal to us as beautiful or ugly, pleasant or unpleasant, stimulating or boring. How astonished some people are when someone else feels quite differently about a particular thing than they do. And how many people there are who judge something on the basis of their own feeling, and on the strength of that consider other people's judgement to be wrong.

The whole welfare society has arisen from the basis that

feeling is focused on the self. Advertising works success-
fully on this principle, and in scientific research greater
significance is often attached to the feeling of personal
achievement than is given to responsibility for the consequences of the discoveries with regard to the future of the
earth and of humankind. In judging other people there is
always the danger that one is swayed by how one feels
oneself with regard to what they say or do and not by how
　　　　　　　　it a possible common task that needs to be
　　　　　　　　ny the other person feels so differently about

　　　　　　　　) have untransformed feelings have no per-
　　　　　　　　of spiritual beings in their environment, or
　　　　　　　　:eive them with reference to themselves, i.e. as
　　　　　　　　npleasant, wonderful or terrible, attractive or
　　　　　　　　according to their state of mind.

　　　　　　　　orm of seduction is that, dependent on their
　　　　　　　　e of health — and usually owing to weak or
damaged bodily organs — people imagine seeing angels or
devils and other spiritual beings everywhere, and do not
notice that these are illusions or distorted images of their
own feelings. These are often also a mixture of illusion and
reality. When the soul is sullied by desires, imaginings,
hidden antipathies or sympathies the spiritual element does
not appear in a pure form but discoloured and darkened.
What applies to the person directly perceiving the messages
applies equally well to all those people obtaining these
messages indirectly. We can put them to the test only with
the aid of transformed feeling accompanied by creative
thinking.

　　How does one acquire transformed feeling? The first
thing you have to do is to give up finding things beautiful or
ugly, good or evil, pleasant or unpleasant. This works best
initially where nature is concerned. You focus on a parti-

cular spot and hold back from applying any thought or explanation to what you see. You simply look at it with feeling until it takes on the form of a small composition. For example three blades of grass, a daisy and a little further away a harebell or a piece of tree bark, a small twig with a red berry on it and white lichen—actually anything can serve to produce true feeling. It has nothing to do with aesthetic dilettantism. This picture-creating feeling can just as well be sparked off by a splash of cow-dung beside some rusty barbed wire or by a stain on a damp wall. If I were to describe a composition which comes about in this way and is unfinished, I would have to bring it into concepts and then it would no longer be alive. I have to look at it, perceive it with my feelings, feel joyful at seeing it, joyful that such a thing exists, surrender fully to the little picture, until the element of thought disappears. And suddenly there is a surge of love. Does it come *from* me? Does it come *towards* me? It is simply there and testifies to the presence of beings which I cannot see with my eyes but which nevertheless, through my releasing my feeling from my own state of comfort, I have liberated from their imprisonment in this little scene. You can compare this experience with something that is known to everybody. I can look at a human eye and concentrate on the colour, the pupil, the white of the eye, the size and the position within the face, i.e. I can limit myself to the outer trappings. I can also look through these various sense perceptions and perceive the soul of a human being or also of an animal, how they feel in themselves, their pain or their joy. The invisible being of the other creature looks at me through the visible eye. This is a mystery which one should not treat lightly, for it opens the gate to love and trust. In this way these natural compositions which we see or hear in a feeling way can become eyes with which we experience their invisible essence. The

same thing happens when we feel our way into the interplay between water, wind and light. Feeling becomes an
organ of perception for other beings. Anyone who practises
this for a considerable while will one day become aware of
the exact moment of transition from the realm of thought to
the realm of loving experience. It is like a very gentle
crossing of the threshold from the sense world to the
supersensible world. You can then begin to carry out
crossings of this kind in other areas too.

Human destiny is the realm in which angels are active.
We focus our inner attention on an episode of our own or of
another person's destiny, similarly to the way we did it with
a segment of nature. And, as then, we renounce all concepts
and psychological explanations and feel our way into it
until it takes on the form of a composition, a small 'piece of
a totality'. It is similar to how a section of a meadow is part
of a whole landscape, and can nevertheless become a
composition, a 'piece of the whole'. Or a sonata can be both
a whole in itself and also a part of the composer's whole
output. People who feel their way into a segment of destiny
in this manner experience the flowing of love, because
beneath the outer trappings of this segment we are coming
into contact with a being, even if we cannot see it ourselves.

Transformation of the will

When people start to transform their thinking and feeling
in this way they will notice that a change is also coming
about in their will. Their thinking is no longer a stringing
together of what they see outside or what they have learnt
at some time or of their opinions about things, but thinking becomes their own individual activity. The unrecog-
nized spiritual principle at work in a plant, in a work of

art and in a person's destiny can be recognized by active thinking. Active thinking makes the invisible visible. Even if we are unaware of it, with this kind of thinking we are actually perceiving the invisible element. Thinking itself acquires the character of will and surrenders itself to what it sets itself to grasp in creative understanding. In the kind of feeling which is a perceiving we hold back our own will. What our will usually does is work into its surroundings. We do something with our hands, with our feet, with our head, and especially with our bodily organs. This has to continue happening, and happens mostly unconsciously. In our perceptive feeling, however, we usually hold back from doing something outwardly. We also renounce our preconceived opinion of what we set ourselves to feel. For the feelings that we relate to our own condition, rather than focusing on the object to be felt, turn into a pronouncement about ourselves and not about the object. If we do not like the scent of a plant, or if we find a work of art either horrible or beautiful, or whether we like a person, all this tells us something about our own condition. Some of us love ginger because it does our liver good. Other people find it unpleasantly sharp and aromatic because they have a different constitution. Some people reject contemporary music, whilst others prefer it, because they are accustomed to listening to different things and to hear them differently. The selfsame person can be admired by some and disapproved of by others, for they have brought different karmic relationships with them into their life. People who are not prepared to dispense either with what they have brought with them or with feelings that refer to themselves — who will not put aside their self-will when facing the phenomena of life — will not be able to transform their feeling into an organ for perceiving the supersensible. However, people who do give up their self-will and in feeling their way into other people get to hear something of their invisible being, acquire a will that does justice to other people, because they understand them. True understanding of the other person's being comes from having a will born of a combination of love and knowing. Understanding is both love and knowing. These two create and receive the transformed will. Anyone can see how differently I am prepared to behave to another person if I imagine I know him or if I love him out of real sympathy as though I understood him apart from sympathy and knowledge. Understanding is a loving form of knowing, a knowing form of loving. It is from these that transformed will arises.

So when thinking becomes creative, when feeling becomes perceptive and when the will is born anew by love and knowing combining to become understanding, then human beings develop the qualities they need to distinguish the different kinds of spirits they themselves experience or other people tell them about. These qualities are impartiality, positivity and equanimity. However, before we have a close look at these three capacities let us consider an objection which could be made to the endeavours just described: Who has the time in the hustle and bustle of life to devote to this sort of thing?

One answer is that we do actually have time for anything that is important to us. A mother of seven children and wife of an artist was once asked how she managed the time to tell her children stories and to paint and play music with them when she did not even have a washing machine or a dishwasher but only a coal range as befitted the insecure basis of her husband's existence. Her reply was: 'The most important thing for me is my children. I would prefer to neglect the household. You have to choose your options.'

Transformation of soul life in the course of daily life

You have to make the choice as to what is most important in life for you. And if we are honest we can often catch ourselves experiencing moments when we are happy enough to be able to put off working on ourselves because we have so many 'important' things to do. Another answer is that we do not necessarily need any extra time for it at all, for there are opportunities enough in daily life to work at it.

A housewife discovered while she was cutting up a red cabbage for dinner what wonderful forms there are inside every head of cabbage. She enjoyed finding them, and she raised them to an artistic level by sticking them on to white cards. They suddenly took on gnomelike features as though they wanted to tell her secrets about the world they had come from. And not only this lady but others who also saw this found the cabbage endearing.

There was a couple who had a severely retarded child. She could move just one hand, slightly, and otherwise communicate only by occasional convulsive screaming, so she had virtually no possibility of expressing herself through her body. With the help of perceptive feeling her parents were able to make contact with the soul of the child. In this way they were able to talk to her and tell her a bedtime story, although there was no outer sign that they were reaching the child. They had the feeling that the following poem [rendered here in prose translation] by Friedrich Schiller gave them an inner image of the child's individuality.

The girl from far away

At the start of each year, with the coming of the first larks, there appeared among poor shepherd folk in a valley a most beautiful girl. Nobody knew whence she came, and all trace of her disappeared as soon as she took her leave. Her presence was a blessing to everyone, and their hearts rejoiced, yet she had a modest dignity which forbade intimacy. She came with flowers and fruits that had ripened in a different land, under a different kind of sunlight where nature was happier. And she made a gift of these fruits and flowers to everyone, both young and old. All were welcomed by her; yet when a loving couple approached, to them she gave the best gifts, the most beautiful flowers of all.

The mother had other children in the family to care for, twins and a further small brother. And the father was extremely caught up in his profession. But the retarded child came to them and needed to be taken seriously, thus giving her parents the chance of cultivating perceptive feeling in life itself. What happened in an extreme case here, however, can happen in any family, even when the mother and father have a great deal to do.

Besides, nearly everyone in our western world has a regular holiday nowadays. What an opportunity this is for the practice of creative thinking, perceptive feeling and, arising from these, the transformation of the will. It takes a while, of course, until you can silence your usual explanatory thinking, your usual feelings of self and the will that reaches out to the surrounding world. Going away with a crowd of other people is hardly suitable for this. Present-day people have first to learn to pause. Because we are normally used to having no time a lot of people find it very difficult to have time. Each biography has its own form, and for some people spending a holiday travelling is just the kind of widening of the horizon they require.

Let us now turn to the requisites which have to be

attained to be able to distinguish nowadays between angel messages and seductions.

Impartiality, equanimity, positivity

If we want to transform our three soul forces this is only possible if we activate three further capacities within ourselves. For instance we cannot think creatively if we say such things as: 'I know what hawthorn is. It has small white blossoms that smell unpleasant. I know John Smith, he is frightfully ambitious and would walk over dead bodies to reach success.' The same applies to thinking that a child with Down's syndrome is destined not to find his place in society. Such judgements are prejudices which prevent the thinking from going through any form of process, even processes in nature, in human beings or in destiny. A bush which has an objectionable smell and appears otherwise to serve no useful purpose is cut down. A person is sized up on the strength of one conspicuous trait which is considered negative. A human destiny is prevented from having the chance to develop and to produce something unexpected. Where this happens the thinking has been swamped by prejudices, people's own state of being becomes the criterion, making them intolerant, spiteful and dismissive of everything that is not pleasant. Their attitude is that they cannot see anything good any more in such plants, such individuals, such destinies, so they react solely negatively. Hedges or other 'disturbers of the peace' in nature are done away with. People are attacked. Destinies are nowadays often cut short in the womb. Yet we can be impartial only if we can devote ourselves to nature, to people and to human destinies unemotionally, patiently and with trust, quite calmly and lovingly.

This kind of attitude can be called equanimity. We are in balance, in our own centre. Human beings can act quite differently from out of this centre. They can now give meaning to or see a meaning in those things they once rejected out of prejudice or self-centredness. They discover that the hawthorn bush shelters birds which not only delight us but also free the fields of pests. They discover that ambitious people grow rich through their many successes and therefore can and do help others. They discover that people with Down's syndrome, if given a welcome in a community, give out an extraordinary amount of heart forces and also receive them from others. In this area too it is life itself that is constantly giving them the possibility to develop and strengthen the three basic soul forces of impartiality, equanimity and positivity. These contribute to the transformation of the three soul forces and become strengthened themselves in the process. We have to make ourselves capable of differentiating between the various kinds of spirits, i.e. of distinguishing whether they are really angels presenting themselves or beings who intend to seduce us. Like the wolf in the Grimm's fairytale 'The Wolf and the Seven Little Kids' who swallowed chalk in order to acquire a voice like the kids' mother, the seductive spirits also assume externally a similar voice to the good ones. The wolf devoured six of the little kids, but not the one that was in the clock case. That one knew the significance of the moment in time. He had presence of mind.

There are various ways in which people acquire these prerequisites for distinguishing spirits. Some people make it their duty consciously to practise one of these basic qualities every day, and also to work regularly at the transformation of their threefold soul life. Other people constantly make a point of responding to the many challenges and spurs to action which life presents. And there are those who already bring these capacities with them into life, in the same way as others bring a musical gift or dexterity in manual skills. They have prepared themselves in earlier lives to work objectively with supersensible experiences.

People who have not transformed their thinking will confront spiritual pronouncements with no discrimination, either with blind belief in miracles or with prejudiced rejection. They know instantly what it says in 'the good book' and compare the two. But just as two thousand years ago the scribes knew all about the Messiah and his enemies, yet when he stood before them they neither recognized him nor themselves, so is it today when people with untransformed thinking do not see that they have spiritual reality in front of them, which just happens to look quite different from how they imagined it on the basis of their 'good book'. How many people are there who read up about a foreign country before they go there and are taken by complete surprise when everything feels so different from what they were given to expect. Only people with impartial creative thinking can distinguish between the 'wolf' and the 'kids' mother' i.e. between their expectations and the genuine thing.

And it is exactly the same with equanimity and perceptive feeling. There are people who hope that messages from the angels will reduce their own problems. Yet when they are told that it is entirely up to themselves to cope with the problem, or they receive no answer at all, their self-esteem is wounded. They will often try to put the blame for the offending messages on to the ones who mediate them. Others will dismiss these messages altogether as the subjective imagination of the receiver, because their own subjective feeling is reacting with fear, and they are scared of the uncomfortable consequences. However, if people examine these messages with transformed feeling and equanimity they will be able to distinguish whether they are a small image of the whole, as described above, or whether they appear unconnected, as though torn out of context, but were masquerading as the whole thing. In the same way, many a sect leader may refer to a heavenly revelation which, though possibly containing a half-truth, is being proclaimed as though it were the epitome of all human striving.

The third quality too is an essential prerequisite for distinguishing between spirits, namely a will that does not want to push itself on to others but is receptive, one that receives the force of positivity and by means of it transforms itself into constructive and loving thinking. With will that has been transformed people see the world differently from before. Without this transformed will they look through rose-coloured spectacles, or they see either black or red. Everyone knows what is meant by these colour comparisons, and everyone will know of a situation when they saw pink, black or red. And how do they see things with a transformed will? Some things they will still see pink, but this will be the case with regard to a process or situation which is genuinely idealistic. For with the aid of rose-tinted spectacles lovers see one another from their best side, but they see only this, and only what they want to see. Yet they do actually see something that is really there. With their transformed will people see the pink part of each other. They also see the black part, but not as being predominant nor definitive. They see it as the expression of the dying process, the death process which everything living must continually go through to live anew.

This is how we practise positivity. These three qualities together, creative, unprejudiced thinking, perceptive, serene feeling and a positive will springing from love, form in us the organ which we call the sense for truth. In the exercising of this sense, knowledge, feeling and good will contribute in an equal measure. This sense is infallible, yet we people of today still have to learn to trust it, both in ourselves and in others. For with this sense explanations, proofs and ordinary logic will not get by.

I had occasion to learn this in the following way. It was the regular practice in our church community that each priest took it in turns to take on the Class I at the local Steiner school for its religion lessons and take that class through to the confirmation. That particular year I knew with this inner sense that although it was not my turn I should nevertheless take on the new Class I. So I searched for reasons with which to convince my colleagues. But the ones I put forward convinced neither them nor myself. So someone else took on the class. Not until six years later did an alteration in the school situation necessitate my taking over that class. It became my 'cross' as I called it, as you can read in my book *What the Angels Need to Tell Us Now*. This showed me clearly that this kind of sense for truth withholds itself from the untransformed soul forces and is built anew from creative thinking, perceptive feeling and the receptive will, and that this sense of truth can be trusted. This is almost more difficult for present-day human beings than the developing of it. This again has its purpose. For over and over again we are challenged to examine what the supersensible experiences are really telling us, and to awaken again and again our sense for truth, which does not function without the openness of the threefold soul.

So if we have the will to distinguish angel messages from the activities of other spiritual beings we have to develop our sense for truth in these three ways, and then learn to trust it. By constantly examining ourselves and working on ourselves in this way we fulfil the first requisite for receiving angel messages and distinguishing them from other kinds.

Let us now look at the second prerequisite.

A communicator of messages from the spiritual world

Right into our own time there are people with so-called second sight, who foresee future events, also events happening a long way away, the death of a close friend.

There are people such as Edgar Cayce, known as the sleeping prophet, who received messages in trance. Seeing what are taken to be events of a past life occurs often through hypnosis or similar practices. Also drugs or bodily influences such as fasting or castigation can transfer people into a state in which they imagine they perceive something spiritual. Many modern artists have received inspiration in this way.

We could continue enumerating methods or states whereby human beings come in touch with a province beyond the senses. However, only a few people are consciously aware of what or with whom they are in touch. For instance the American writer Henry Miller describes in his book *Big Sur and the Oranges of Hieronymus Bosch* how he often felt compelled to sit down at his typewriter and write things he found very unpleasant.

So, among all the many possibilities practised and passed on by people nowadays, how can we know for certain that what is seen or put into words is really of angelic origin and not something pathological, untimely or misleading? Even in ordinary life there are certain features which can show us, if we are open enough and well practised, whether we are dealing with a person who is talking absolutely out of him or herself, purely out of their own unspoilt being. For one thing there is the look in their eyes. For another thing there is the voice and the way they speak. Children are still absolutely natural, for the harmony between their souls and their angel is still undisturbed. How deep and searching can be the gaze of children in the first months of life. And how open and radiant they are right up to about the ninth year of life, except in certain situations when they leave their angel.

One of the probationers working with me in my Class 3 had a watch stolen which he had put down on the table. When I was shaking each child by the hand as I always did as they left the classroom one of the boys could not look me in the eye as he usually did. This aroused in me the suspicion that he was the one who had taken the watch. I had already endeavoured, unsuccessfully, to provide an opportunity for the likely little thief to return the watch. In the following lesson he came to me and told me he was a watch collector (which was in fact true) and he had found in his collection a watch which looked exactly like that of the probationer. He would like to give it to him to replace the stolen one. I accepted this. It was the stolen one, of course, but I did not say anything in front of the class. When the children left I arranged things so that he was the last to leave. I detained him for a moment and told him: 'You and I know the real story about the watch. It is important that we do. The angels know it too. You and I know the truth about the stolen watch.' From that moment on he could look me in the eye again.

I have sometimes had the experience with grown-ups that suddenly the look in their eyes changed so rapidly it seemed as though another being was looking at me, usually an evil one. In the case of people on the point of death it was, on the other hand, often a look of release. When one meets a person again after decades whom one knew in their youth the expression in the eyes is often the only thing by which one recognizes them. It is through the gaze that people's individuality looks at us, and this is either connected with their angel or not. It is similar with the voice. We recognize one another by our voices and our way of speaking. Some people speak breathlessly, or they constantly insert 'umm' and 'er'. Some people stammer and others speak so that it sounds put on, as though they wanted to be someone other than they are. The way people speak reveals how they confront themselves, whether they match up to their true being. People who continually re-establish this state of being in tune with themselves are at the same time in tune with their angels. And if it is in accordance with their angels, i.e. if it belongs to the prenatal arrangement between them and their angel, it will be in their destiny to perceive angels in earthly life, to have their eyes opened to the realm beyond the sense world.

Rudolf Steiner once said that we do many things in life which we only come to understand much later on. And he went on to say that when we make a discovery of this nature then this moment of discovery awakens the following feelings within us: We feel as though protected by a good power which is at work within the depths of our own being. We begin to have more and more trust in the fact that actually, in the best sense of the word, we are not alone in the world, and that everything we can grasp and everything we can do consciously is basically only a small part of what we accomplish in the world.* This spells out quite clearly that our angel pervades our individual being. And when the angels want to make themselves known they have to make use of a person's individual language. Art, music and

---

*See Rudolf Steiner, *The Spiritual Guidance of the Individual and Humanity*, Anthroposophic Press, 1992.

lyric poetry can be such a language, but so can every form of action which they have helped us to arrive at by way of inspiration or intuition.

Messages sent by good beings, and which are therefore in keeping with present times, also have the characteristic that the people who act as mediators do not deplete their physical forces in order to make their spiritual forces stronger, but that meditation and prayer are carried out to strengthen the spiritual forces, and the body serves as an instrument. These people do not withdraw from present-day life by going into a monastery or a convent or into a remote part of the world untouched by technology or human problems in order to live their lives, as happened in former times. A further characteristic showing that someone is in the service of good angels is that they do not use their messages to exert pressure of any kind, as is frequently the case.

A mother and father who came to me for advice had had the following experience: Their seventeen-year-old son lay in intensive care with a fracture at the base of his skull. His mother applied for help from a person who could guide them in healing through prayer. In addition she made an oath that if her son came through and was allowed to live she would either adopt a Vietnamese child or sponsor an adoption. Her son recovered. The boy's father objected to an adoption because he foresaw that his wife would be overtaxed and not be able to do the child justice. Despite this the healer wanted to persuade the woman to go through with the adoption, and told her that he was able to perceive the soul of the child who was already counting on coming. In this dilemma I advised the mother not to let herself be influenced by anybody, neither by her husband nor by the healer, but to decide for herself, in freedom, what she was capable of taking on. She decided to take on the sponsorship, for she felt she was too old to bring up a small child all over again, now that her own children were almost grown-up. She was afraid to do it. In this way she freed herself from the compelling power of the message given her by a clairvoyant. For me, this occurrence was a sign that it is not enough to have supersensible faculties, for if one is working in the service of the angels it is essential to leave the other person free.

The following is an example showing the opposite of the above. A woman asked Agnes to enquire of the angels whether and how she could help a friend in the throes of a difficult life crisis. She was told that she could send him good thoughts; the angels described how things were with him, and that he should learn to make different use of his capacities. However, she should not tell him this. Otherwise he would do it because the angels say so, and it was particularly important in his case that he change his life entirely out of his own freewill. One can read from this that the unselfish mediator has no intention of playing a part or having any influence where her messages are concerned, but puts herself at the service of the angels and human beings to help create a connection which is spiritually in keeping with the times. She clothes her messages in a straightforward language and attaches great significance to a full comprehension of other people's questions. For it all passes through her clear, wide-awake consciousness, with the thoughts she brings into words being formed not from sense perceptions but from supersensible perceptions. This is why the language of her messages is simple and human and springs from her very own being. It is no literal dictation written down when she is not in possession of her own human consciousness.

Surely the most difficult part of it for the human beings who receive messages is that they have to refrain from adding anything of their own to them. Any opinion they might have about a question asked, and preconceived ideas or emotional response, wishes, hopes, even anything the slightest bit shady, and of which they are often totally unaware, must first be silenced. Agnes, for example, pictures this process of purification as a process of immersing herself successively in baths of different coloured water which liberate her from subjective thoughts and feelings so that they subsequently leave her free. With areas which reach far beyond the questions and problems of individual people and which have to do with the future of humankind or of what individual people and groups of people are doing for a future in connection with the divine plan, Agnes feels as though a sheltering cloak is wrapped round her which is removed after the messages have been delivered. For it is obvious that misanthropic beings are interested in disturbing such processes or distorting their content. Sometimes she is even afforded this protection by several angels who surround her for days, install themselves before the questions begin and only depart after a while. As confirmation, and also to give her inner strength, she is sometimes told that she has played her part satisfactorily and carried out the task well. For she constantly puts the sources of the messages to the test. However, she developed the above described sense of truth a long time ago. If there is part of the message she does not understand she persists with questioning until it is clear. Much of it is given in images whose meaning is usually included at the same time. But sometimes the meaning becomes clear only when she makes further enquiry.

It is this persistent questioning which enables her to find the solution to problems which are initially incomprehensible to her. Thus persistence and testing on her part, and an understanding on the part of all the people involved, is an important criterion in our time for cooperating in this way with angels. That they continually expect this distinguishes their messages from those of seductive spiritual beings.

Angels and their adversaries can be distinguished by their behaviour

In St Luke's Gospel (I.19) we are shown how an angel, on appearing to a doubting human being, announces himself by name. He tells the priest Zacharius: 'I am the angel Gabriel who stands in the presence of God.' Nowadays the angels also announce themselves to those who see them either by name or by a symbol or by the atmosphere which surrounds them. The adversaries, on the other hand, do not want to be recognized. And if they are nevertheless recognized they can become very aggressive.

I was once witness to someone telling a close friend that he was of the opinion that much of what the friend said and did did not originate from himself at all, but that another being was acting and speaking through him. It took place in a quiet restaurant, and it seemed a good moment for a heart-to-heart talk. But as soon as the words had been uttered the eyes of the person being addressed had a sharp look in them, a malicious spark. The man became very aggressive, lashed out with wounding remarks, then got up and went, without continuing the journey they were undertaking together. Much later on, when they were all in their own homes again, this happening was discussed, and the man in question thanked his friend, and said that he had not realized before what was the cause of the recurrent feeling of being at odds with himself, both with respect to social relationships and in the practice of his art. For he was an artist. Although this destructive element continued to arise in him, he was now prepared to recognize it as a foreign influence, and it gradually disappeared. It is like Rumpelstiltskin, whose name nobody knows. But when it is discovered and he is addressed by it, his aggression turns back on himself, and he tears himself to pieces.

More often than in individuals, we encounter in broader contexts these beings who do not want to be recognized. Not wanting to reveal their real names they make use of the acronyms so popular today. And because they realize that human beings are finding them more and more useful — are in fact becoming addicted to this service, because it makes them rich, successful or merely fascinates them, puts them under its spell — they play a joke on them now and again and express their nature in an abbreviation of this kind. For instance there was an advertisement for satellite antennae which was sent out as an attractively illustrated circular put through every letterbox. The words 'satellite antennae' were abbreviated to Sat-An, satan. Does anyone recognize what is hiding behind such inventions? If they do, they will endeavour to put the being behind this name in *their* service, and release themselves from having to serve it.

The angels do not of course speak a human language yet they make themselves known and speak to us. How is this? There are also earthly creatures who speak no human language and yet speak to us — have something to say to us. We can experience this with every plant, animal and landscape. We say that we 'listen to a dandelion speaking to us', meaning that we build up its being within ourselves, in the way we have described creative thinking, which causes it to make its being more and more describable in our language, or rather we draw its being into our language. It is the same with everything the sense world shows us. In the case of the angels it is the other way round. They build up the invisible part of our being within themselves, until they bring to expression the unuttered part of us. Similarly the name of our angel also lives, unuttered, in us, and he can then reveal it himself in our human language. The time spirit, Michael, too, can speak within us if we open ourselves to him; also other angels, if a human being lets them create an image of him within themselves. This only happens if he lets them look at him without evading them, without feigning false facts about himself.

Some people may think that an angel always sees them as they are, even when they recoil from accepting the truth about their own being. This is so. But if human beings want to perceive angels they themselves must allow them to create their image and to speak within them in the same way as human beings get nature to speak within them. Then a variation of the wise words of Oetinger comes to expression: 'The eye with which God sees me is the same eye with which I see God.' We can also say: 'The ears with which the angels hear me are the same as the ears with which I hear the angels.' Or: 'The language of my true being speaking within an angel is the same one as an angel speaks in me.' This is how we human beings come to know the name, the being, the power that is the angel wanting to speak and make himself known to us.

When we grasp this relationship between angels and human beings we can then understand why so many of the angels' messages make us feel: Actually, I already knew that! We realize that we have already had a similar thought or inkling. Then the suspicion can easily arise that the receiver of the messages was influenced telepathically by the person asking the questions. However, this person recognizes that this is not so through the fact that the content is not the same on the intellectual level but has to work its way from the feelings into thought form. In fact it is often the case that one first of all experiences it as a total contradiction to what one has oneself come across. Not until one has thought about or meditated for some time on the angel's message does one realize that the answer is giving one a key to a completely new way of seeing and understanding such things. And I experience deep down that an answer of this kind, which is at first totally alien to me, is actually something I already knew but was reluctant to accept. Or the outer demeanour of a person hid the inner situation, or I would not let it come home to me because its consequences were unpleasant.

The messages are only telepathic if they convey the untransformed thoughts and feelings of the questioner. In that case the contact arises out of the everyday consciousness which is experienced as something much shallower than the feeling of confirmation arising out of the depths of the soul. This is how it is. Thus the influences or messages that pass on a spiritual level between human being and human being, between adversaries and human beings or angels and human beings are clearly distinguishable. The essential criteria are: whether the questions arise out of love towards what is being asked, whether the answers leave people free, and whether there is a conscientious feeling for truth in both the person who asks the questions and the person who answers.

Human dignity – angelic dignity

What do we mean when we speak of human dignity or of something being worthy of a human being? We certainly know very well what being unworthy of a human being means. Conditions are unworthy of a human being if people lack the basic needs of life, such as a roof over their heads, food, sleep, health care, freedom of thought and of belief, work, education etc., etc. If their dignity is being respected they should be treated neither as animals nor as a machine. This type of human dignity should be generally accorded to everyone. There are, over and beyond this, people who radiate a special kind of dignity independent of their position, vocation or other outer circumstances.

When I was doing the practical part of my training for the priesthood I was asked to acquaint myself with a group of people who lived in the workers' part of the town. I came into a parlour kitchen where there were a number of people engaged in discussing a talk they had heard. There was just one person who said nothing but listened attentively to what the others said. He made an impression on me because, sitting modestly in the corner of a sofa, he radiated tremendous goodness and dignity. After a while one of the participants in the discussion asked him to tell them what he thought about the theme. So he began to speak gently. All the others listened to him very quietly. The atmosphere in the room changed. I had the feeling that an angel might enter now, for each one of the others could discover himself in what 'Father Goessel' was saying. Father Goessel was a foreman in a textile factory and also the counsellor to everybody from unskilled labourer to director. His own human dignity prepared others for the dignity of the power of destiny, of the angels. And it was his awareness of the dignity of angels which gave him this superior human dignity.

How can we human beings awaken and cultivate in ourselves this consciousness of the dignity of angels? To start with, by cultivating an awareness of human dignity, and not only towards people whom we like and who are close to us but also with regard to people who make life difficult for us. They also possess human dignity, but it has become buried to a great extent because the people around them have never addressed it, cultivated or nourished it. If you accord human dignity to people who appear so utterly mindless by not only supplying them outwardly with conditions worthy of a human being but paying particular attention to respecting their inner being, even though this is hidden and buried in a distorted form, you are acquiring the ability to see with the eyes of angels, even if you are not conscious of this. It shows itself in a kind of love enabling you to grow beyond all the antipathy, rejection and condemnation stemming from nature or your own feelings.

If we want to be equal to the task of according an angel his angelic dignity we must treat him with human dignity, i.e. be humble but upright, open and trusting towards what is still not understood, silent in wordless speech. Angels like being greeted, and they greet human beings on approaching them. They need our trust in that they enter not only into our body but into our soul. They love being thanked, because the act of thanking maintains the connection between them and the human being. Greeting them, having trust in them and thanking them are expressions of human dignity which make us worthy of the angels. Whether human beings perceive angels clairvoyantly and report their presence to others, or whether it is through their own soul that they receive thoughts, feelings and impulses for life in such a manner that they sense the activity of angels because they are 'lifted above themselves', in every case the sort of inner dignity is necessary which is not replaceable by external measures. We can light a candle, look at a picture or listen to impressive music, burn a joss-stick or organize a festive meal. None of this replaces an attitude of human dignity towards the dignity of the angels, though it may be helpful. In no way can angels be called up by applying technicalities such as are customary in spiritualistic seances. If the receiving of messages is to happen without disturbance and distortion the atmosphere has to be pure. By saying the Lord's Prayer—as long as we are moved by it and do it with intense feelings and not parrot fashion—we can purify the atmosphere for receiving angels, so that both image and sound reach our soul clearly. This purification can also be achieved by means of any spiritual revelation such as the Gospels or a verse given by an initiate, or a sacrament. Through any of these things we can bring about union with our angel.

The content of angel messages

Angels never appeal to human egotism, as happens so often today in the case of other spirits. I continually receive letters from spiritual seers promising all kinds of things on the basis of their ability to see into the future and to prophesy karmic involvements awaiting me. They tell people when to expect good fortune, money, favourable relationships etc., and what they should be wary of. And for this they expect a corresponding financial remuneration. When someone with supersensible faculties of whatever kind wants to earn money all the time, that is a sign that the content does not come from 'worthy' beings. Angel messages help people, either by giving them knowledge or comfort. Sometimes they prepare a person to face difficult situations. Some people, if they are mature enough, can be shown a mirror in which to see themselves as the angel sees them. Angels can even ask human beings for help, because they themselves cannot reach into the earthly realm like human beings do, as we heard in a previous message: '... we are "only" angels.'* They neither judge us nor moralize the way we do, but always behave in such a way that we become alerted to

---

*What the Angels Need to Tell Us Now, p. 94.

what is in store for us. If it is of benefit to a person's eternal being they will also lead us into what we would call misfortune or difficulty, sometimes even into evil. But we receive this in message form only subsequently. In any case it shows a total lack of relationship to or knowledge of the angel world to maintain that if a so-called misfortune happens to oneself or someone else it is because the angel was not paying attention. It was rather that the human being was not paying attention and failed to notice what the angel had to tell him.

The angels are servants of Christ. There are nine hierarchies of angels. The tenth is humankind, which will one day have become fully human. We may already call ourselves human beings, but in the eyes of heaven we are still on the way to becoming what we were created for, namely to become the image of God. Humankind would have totally lost this impulse to become human if the God of Creation had not himself become a human being. By his voluntary deed he awakened anew in humankind the impulse to become human. Since then he lives as the impulse to become human in every individual person, whether we are aware of this or not. Pilate recognized this correctly when he pointed to Christ, crowned with thorns, and said the words: 'Ecce homo, that is a human being.' We can recognize the messages coming from angels who serve Christ in that these angels are in the service of the Christian path, irrespective of which faith we adhere to. What is characteristic of the human path is not the desire for more and more possessions but rather a brotherly handling of possessions, the endeavour to acquire equal rights for everyone instead of the exercising of power, and love which encompasses suffering, death and evil, just as Christ did on his human path, so as to transform these into aids along the way. We can recognize angel messages by the help they bring to our becoming human. Anything that promises possessions, power or love as a reward, comes from another direction.

Angels' messages do not contradict logic, the wisdom of nature, nor love, as the messages from other beings do. They are, to quote the Church Father Augustine, only 'against nature as we know it'. We could add, against the sort of logic that is restricted to cause and effect, and against the kind of love which wants to keep hold of things and is afraid of change. This is how we can learn from the very content of angel messages to distinguish them from those of other beings. They serve the human path and thereby Christ in us.

The different ranks and tasks of spiritual messengers

At all times in the history of humankind there have been initiates who, whilst incarnated on earth, could live in the spiritual world to such an extent that they could bring down from spirit realms impulses giving direction and advice right into the social conditions in agriculture, animal husbandry, education and the healing of illness in a form suitable for human evolution in those times. Such initiates exist to this day. For western culture one of these was Rudolf Steiner. It is clear from his autobiography that already as a child he possessed spiritual faculties that were evidence of his great mission, and which enabled him to see what others could not see in his human environment. Only his geometry teacher, and later on a herb gatherer, testified to the fact that the spiritual world can be known to all kinds of human beings in the most diverse of ways. He entered more and more fully into the life of his time, studied at the technical college, had contact with all layers of society, and so fulfilled the task his spiritual teachers had given him of 'slipping under the skin of the dragon', to experience from inside the all-prevailing materialism. He tells us in his autobiography about everything that prepared him in his childhood and youth, as an initiate, to renew culture in the broadest sense.* In his own time only a small number of people took up this impulse. Even today it is not a large number. Yet its effect today is immense and is seeping very gently into the lives of many people.

Those people who have taken up the impulses brought by this initiate and have begun to bring them into their lives are not able themselves to be active in the spiritual world in the realm of research as Rudolf Steiner was. And yet we could call them spiritual researchers. On the foundation of the messages brought by the initiate they carry out research in the realm where the spiritual element manifests itself in the sense world. Along these lines researchers have developed picture-forming methods, those of capillary dynamolysis, blood crystallization and drop pictures with which they have shown evidence of the life force or formative force in various substances. Researches of this kind, in which discoveries have been made showing the activity of supersensible forces in the sense realm, have taken place in many domains.

There are also people with varying degrees of clairvoyance. These have to be distinguished from initiates. They can bring messages from the spiritual world and indications, thoughts and ideas given by an initiate to people who are not clairvoyant, to help them acquire an ever better understanding of what they perceive with their senses, and to distinguish who it is who is bringing them messages. It is often those people mentioned aboved, who do research into spiritual matters, who are able to help them. For what they

---

*See *Autobiography*, Anthroposophic Press, 1999.

are seeking is confirmation of whether what they are experiencing is both real and sound.

We can all discover, as well, that we by no means perceive physical things only with our bodily senses. Are we not able to perceive someone else's joy and pain, even if they do not show them externally? And when we enter a room are we not able to perceive the emotional atmosphere there? And the spiritual content in art, music and poetry, are we not able to perceive these? And cannot we often perceive, too, if someone is thinking about us? Or if a dear friend, a long way away, is not well? Our life is full of such spiritual perceptions. It is only that we are usually too weak to bring them to consciousness because they come and go so quickly that they cannot be made to stay. We could say that clairvoyance is a heightened awareness which sees through the visible world to the occurrences constantly happening in the invisible realm. So our physical eye can be described very aptly as a physical/physiological apparatus, but that what looks through the eye is of a supersensible nature. When we discover the connecting link between initiates, spiritual researchers, people who are clairvoyant and those who reach through to the supersensible realm through its sense exterior we shall be able to confirm that it would be to great advantage if these people were to achieve ever fuller cooperation.

Dealing with angel messages

Angel messages have been written down in this book chapter by chapter. But this is not the way they were given. There were always longer or shorter gaps in between. The questions arose for actual reasons, and the answers need to be thought about for some time. They often appear to be quite simple. Their deeper dimension opens up only if we do not immediately judge them, i.e. measure them against what we previously considered right, but let them work on our sense for truth in an unbiassed way, and live with them by looking at them unhurried again and again.

We could take the statements about psychotherapy and biography work as examples to show that these answers given us by angels need considerable reflection. At the first reading we may not agree with them, and not until we make the effort to follow through the train of thought do we understand what is meant. We have of course first of all to learn to think in paradoxes, especially when the answer begins with 'Yes and no'. Only by reading it very carefully and thinking about it from all sides do we come to realize that 'the angels are moving among us human beings'.

May the following angel messages help us to realize this. They can give us advice and information about various matters that present problems to us today, the unsolved and unredeemed ones, and the things that upset us and make us insecure. May the reading of these chapters be of help in this way.

Part II

MESSAGES ON CONTEMPORARY ISSUES

Donating and receiving organs

As we know, there are very great differences of opinion about organ transplantation. Just as with blood, the population is being increasingly asked to donate organs. Many organ transfers considered possible from a medical point of view, and which would lengthen someone's life, cannot be carried out because the required organ is not available. In an attempt to reduce this shortage laws may be introduced to the effect that organs can be removed from people unless they have in full consciousness put down in writing that in the event of brain death they are against the removal of an organ.

Reports from people who have been given an organ transplant are diametrically opposed. Some of them are happy that they are still alive. A few even resolve to give a totally new form to this new life they have been given, making it into a life of service to others, or one that is more spiritually orientated, or one in which they are constantly aware of tremendous gratitude. Others feel very strongly that life is a torment, that they are alienated from themselves. Even those around them hardly recognize them any more. We can also ask whether life after death changes to the detriment of donors. If their heart or their kidneys live on in the organism of another person do they remain attached to these in some way? And have doctors got the right to take such drastic steps to prolong the life of a human being whose hour of death has struck? Is it permissible to interfere in this way in a person's destiny which was pre-ordained and chosen by that individual before birth? I am not the only one who thinks about these questions. Many people in my environment do.

Agnes and I, together, raised all these questions with a doctor who constantly had to deal with such problems in connection with her practice. We were particularly concerned about the question of what the consequences of donating an organ are on the after-death existence of a donor. Valuable points of view of the following kind show the angel perspective:

In principle there are no consequences for the donor in the life after death, as the soul and the human individuality as such remain untouched by what happens to the physical body. For instance, many people, through war or a serious accident, lose a limb or it is destroyed, yet they can go on their 'regular' after-death journey. At death the soul detaches itself completely from the body, even in the case of the heart of the deceased being implanted into another person. The soul forces follow the normal path. Nevertheless the organs themselves are bound up with qualities which have been strongly marked by the individual characteristics of the previous owner. We could say that every organ is governed by a particular personal star, its 'signature'; it has, so to speak. the individual's vibrations. By way of these vibrations the receiver of the organ is influenced on a precise level. We have to presume that this, as well as the fact of what organ the receiver gets, has been karmically intended. Friction can actually arise between the vibrations of the donated organ and the organism of the receiver, both in the realm of the body as well as of the soul. However, the task of balancing out karma can nevertheless go ahead.

This theme is extremely complicated, and it is very difficult to give answers which apply in general, as the various instances depend on individual karma. For example if a recipient has acquired the heart of someone who had very negative vibrations then he has to take up as a life task the struggle against the negativity. Yet it could be the case that if he had not received this donated heart this challenge would have come his way from another direction. So karma certaintly decides who gets which organ; it is certainly not a matter of chance. Thus the angels who accompany human destinies also include in their guidance the modern possibilities of prolonging life. In their view the fact of donating an organ has no effect on the next incarnation of the donor, just as little as does the distribution of his organs among various recipients. But it can be the case that the vibrations of the donated organ – as already presented – can have consequences for the further life of the various recipients.

The part of the doctor who carries out the removal and transplantation of the organ was also considered. The doctor ought to know what kind of part he is playing when, after so-called brain death, he removes an organ from someone still alive. What he is doing here is not the same as merely exchanging or inserting spare parts. He has to muster the proper ethical respect. Otherwise it would be better if he had become a mechanic. The moral attitude with which he performs the task of removing and transplanting the organ of course also has its karmic effects and consequences both for those immediately affected as well as for the karmic set-up of everyone involved. It is not the case, as is often presumed, that the angels see this as a killing. The doctor is only the instrument performing the operation and he has placed himself at the service of science, and transplantations happen nowadays to be part of this service. One can ask oneself whether the prolongation of life through organ transplantation is God's will. To this the angels say that such factors may certainly be part of the divine plan for our lives. Thus these people have the chance of living a further stretch of life with the aid of another organ, but they have to cope with the effects and limitations resulting from this.

I remembered having heard the account of a leading surgeon who, prior to every scheduled transplant operation, experiences the presence of a form of light of whom he enquires whether it is part of the patient's destiny to go through with this operation and its consequences. The answer varies. He endeavours only to perform the transplantation if the angel has consented. Sometimes, however, as he cannot of course speak to his scientifically-minded colleagues about angels, he finds himself forced to operate without the angel's consent. In answer to the question as to what that signified for him himself, he said he would have to pay for it with his life. A short while later he lost his life in an unusual way. The destiny of that doctor confirms what the angels said. It made me think of the Grimm's fairytale of Godfather Death. If the doctor saw Death standing near the head of the patient's bed he was permitted to cure him. If he saw Death near his feet he would not be able to do so. On being called to the King's daughter who was sick unto death he saw Death standing at her feet. Because it was a matter of honour, and also the King's daughter had been promised him as his bride if he could cure her, he lifted her up and turned her round so that Death after all was standing at her head. The princess became well. But Death led the doctor to a cave where the sparks of the lives of every human being were shining. His was almost burnt out, and he knew that he would die very soon, and he also knew why.

We continued our conversation with the angels and asked about the consequences for recipents of organs. Do they share the responsibility for the donor's loss of organs? We were told:

'Yes and no. Through consciously deciding to receive an organ the recipient also bears responsibility for this, of course. In fact, one is often not sure whose organ one is having to live with. Even the recipients have the attitude of making use of a store of spare parts. But sometimes, through the pain and suffering of the operation, a new outlook arises.'

We wondered whether the course of destiny was planned this way. And again we received the answer that both were thought of. 'Yes, of course. There are always several ways.'

We asked whether any obligations arise towards the donor. 'No, it is more the other way round. If people express a readiness to become an organ donor they feel responsible after their death for having to balance something out. Even if it is only to do with a physical organ like this. This balancing out can involve either positive or negative radiations for the recipient. It depends on the karmic connection. Obligations towards the donor do not arise, because what needs to be balanced out is a karmic matter.'

When we asked how we could know whether a transplantation was karmic or not, we were told that every operation lay in the hands of God. If it is successful it is his Will, if it is 'apparently' unsuccessful, then that is the way.

We went on to ask that if the whole transplantation business is accepted and necessary, how far may our research go if the results are not foreseeable?

'No, the whole range of medicine existing at present is not acceptable or necessary. It is the human beings who want it. We can cope with it at present. But it has already gone too far. For doctors think they are all-powerful. They can create life and destroy it. Apparently. But now is not the time to talk about this. To close, we want to say once again that judgements about organ transplantation vary very much from case to case. The main problem lies with the recipient.'

All these answers can help us to understand why organ transplantation is experienced and judged so differently by different people, and how important it is that the decision is undertaken both by the recipient as well as by the donor in full consciousness and freedom.

Gene technology

Now that we know that the whole process of organ transplantation can be thought of as part of the wisdom of karmic connections, the question arises whether there is a similar positive possibility for gene research, too. This, however, is not the case: 'As long as people put their trust only in what can be proved by physics and chemistry, and as long as they pay no attention, either in their research or in their daily lives, to the forces that give matter its life and form, they are hardly likely to notice any difference between plants that have been forced or even gene-manipulated and put into food and those that merely fill the stomach but do nothing for the forces of life and of health in the human organism. A great many illnesses arise from this unbalanced diet, which is then supplemented by vitamins and minerals in the form of tablets. A diet that does not stimulate the living, formative forces in plants, animals and human beings has its effect right into psychology and social relations.'

Some time ago I heard a lecture in which the speaker, a doctor by profession, talked about today's social problems, difficulties in understanding one another, feeling isolated, starting relationships and not keeping them going, and that these problems had to do with our diet. Our food may fill our stomach, but it has no life force any longer to support our humanity. A human being no longer sends out a radiation, creates an atmosphere which can pass from one soul to another. Today, people are a lot like a cat that has been thrown into water. When it comes out its fur no longer crackles when we stroke it, it no longer sends out sparks, forming an aura of energy. It is as thin as a rat and radiates nothing.

I remembered this when the angels answered our question regarding what happens to the life forces of plants, animals and human beings in the case of genetically-modified food.

'The life forces in them are weak, and when a human being eats such products his individuality also becomes weak. For there is no spiritual strength in them. They may have the ability to feed people but not the ability to have any effect. One can certainly speak of the dark forces which are endeavouring more and more to increase their power by these means. When they weaken both human beings and nature it makes them feel good. But one must admit that even without gene technology there is enough food around today that has little strength in it. And yet, looked at from a spiritual perspective, it still has quite a different colour than genetically-modified food. Gene technology, no doubt, does not conform to positive spiritual standards but it belongs to the present time. Human beings have a great deal of knowledge in their hands. They think they can produce new life. This kind of life has no strength but is illusive, unreal, empty. Yet to start with they do not notice this. The flowers their hands produce have the same beautiful forms as those that have "grown naturally". They dazzle them. They are an illusion.

'Even individuals who acquire their existence through a

process of selection lack the force to develop this individuality in conformity with their spiritual potential. A lot could be said on this theme, but the times are not yet ready for it.

'It is quite a different matter when two people love one another and are really attached to one another. Then fertilization outside the mother's body can find blessing, provided, of course, that the sperm is his sperm, and the ovum her ovum. They share the suffering that has to be endured until this child can at last incarnate. But this is not so in principle. In the case of women who want a child and make use of a sperm donor, it is a misuse of it. That people manipulate a human being so that it will be born with the qualities they choose is not in accordance with our way of thinking.

'Present-day researchers are convinced of their power to do anything it is possible to do. But they do not understand the world. They have not chosen their profession for nothing. There has always been this type of person, but they were previously in other spheres of influence. These gene researchers have no connection to the spirit in nature.'

This phase in history will come to an end. Today it gives the impression that gene technology will continue to grow and cover more and more areas. It is increasing now, but it will decrease again. For the time will come when people will realize how contrary to nature it is. If it were to continue to increase, the destruction of the earth would follow.

Gene technology is justified only in order to recognize or cure illnesses but not purely for the sake of producing an impeccable line of heredity.

Readers will no doubt have had thoughts along the same lines as these messages about gene technology, but I find it comforting to know that its time will pass.

Cloning human beings

If science does not shrink from cloning human beings then there will be big questions, such as whether cloned 'people' are beings with an ego, and whether the divine wisdom of the world will permit the cloning of human beings at all.

Before we can understand the angels' way of looking at this we must clarify the difference between soul and spirit. Then we shall be better able to deal with the answer. The soul lives in the spheres of thinking, feeling and the will. The spirit (the ego) is the individual kernel of each human being. As individual beings we operate in the three spheres of the soul, interpenetrate them and endeavour to govern them according to our destiny. We live in our destiny, even if it appears to encounter us from outside. A soul without an ego can be interpenetrated and governed by other beings. It lacks the commitment to the wisdom of pre-natal decisions which the individuality establishes in harmony with its angel, the spiritual companion along the path of destiny. Our question arose out of concern that such things can happen, and received in answer:

'This cloning goes against the natural course of life. Dark powers make certain souls suitable to inhabit cloned material. They are torn out of normal after-death evolution. They have to be instantly available. These beings certainly have a soul. But this soul is by no means ready for earthly life. It is contrary to the divine plan, contrary to all reason. These torn-out souls find it very difficult to fall into line. They would certainly have morality but they would have no ego and therefore would not have a path of life ahead of them which they had chosen before birth. There will be attempts — there have been attempts already — to "produce" cloned human beings. The temptation to play "creator" is for some scientists irresistible, the feeling of power too great. The threshold of restraint was passed a long time ago. It will be attempted. But this attempt, involving the tearing out of souls, is like a lacerated wound caused by a beast of prey. It disturbs the balance of the earth. And eventually this beast of prey will turn against its creator. It will tear out parts of his own inner being.'

This means that people who clone human beings will themselves become the prey of the 'raging tiger' and will lose the wholeness of their individual being, their ego. Rudolf Steiner describes evil beings whom he calls asuras and who tear out pieces of the human ego. The image of the raging tiger put me in mind of this.

The causes and effects of BSE

In 2000 and 2001 people's state of mind in Europe received a tremendous shock through the fact that so-called mad cow disease broke out on many farms which, passed on to human beings, leads to terrible forms of illness. Many animal lovers were horrified when thousands of cattle were culled prophylactically, as this kind of killing is called. Initially it appeared that right up to ministry level people were going to wake up to the fact that animals cannot be allowed to be treated as lifeless goods solely for profit but must be dealt with according to their proper nature as creatures with life and soul. In many instances people's attitude to consumerism changed. They no longer bought beef, often no other kind of meat either. Scientists searched for a virus which could have triggered off the illness. Very few drew attention to the fact that animals living entirely on a plant diet are bound to get ill, even to go mad, if they are fed fodder containing animal ingredients. It goes against their nature as cattle.

As happens so often, this almost hysterical reaction passed, and very few conclusions have yet been arrived at with regard to it. Perhaps it would be different if people were to take seriously information offered from spiritual insight. Therefore we shall quote it here:

'These animal souls who were slaughtered in their thousands were sent to earth as a large homogeneous whole. They are very important for the life of the earth and of humankind. Hardly anyone suspects today what cows signify for all earthly creatures. Then it happens that these animals are not allowed to follow the natural course of their lives and their spiritual purpose but are prevented through lunacy from doing so. This lunacy arises in the human brain. In the spiritual world only this spiritual lunacy in the human brain is visible, meaning that these people cannot be proved to be physically ill but only their thinking is ill. Then this illness is projected on to the animals. Through human lunacy it is now the animals who really become physically ill. And human lunacy is increased even further through the fact of culling these masses of cattle. Yet the origin of the madness is still in the human brain. (What is meant by lunacy is wrong thoughts.) People think that by murdering the apparently sick animals they are temporarily relieving the burden on the earth. But this removal leads to imbalance and works against the spirit of nature.

'When, after death, the animals return to the soul world they do not take the unhealthy element along with them. They leave that on earth. For what is ill does not go into the soul world. It is precipitated on to the earth. The ill factor will only be cured if people treat the ground properly. Otherwise it will get into the food chain again, not as BSE but in a different form. The imbalance left behind in the human world by the slaughtering of the animals is far greater than the one created by the sudden return of the animals into the spiritual world. In the supersensible world there are not these great imbalances such as exist in the human world.'

Using nuclear energy

In today's society there are opponents of nuclear energy and supporters of it worldwide. The one group sees the danger it poses for the life of humankind and the earth. The other sees the benefit and the material profit this form of energy brings to people and believes that the danger can be kept in check. In reality it is no longer merely a matter of the clash between benefit and danger, for nuclear power stations have been functioning for decades and the so-called nuclear waste, which has allegedly been taken care of so that it can no longer be dangerous, already radiates into the earth; and many regions which are already radioactive will continue to be so for endless ages. Is there a further view beyond these two conflicting attitudes? We were shown two aspects which extend our horizon regarding the occurrences following on the discovery of nuclear energy.

One aspect is that dealing with nuclear energy demands the greatest discipline. As long as the people who have to do with nuclear energy put the desire for gain above morality it is not possible to use this energy responsibly. The already existing nuclear power stations require great care and attention. People who do not have respect for this energy should not work in this area. In principle nuclear energy is something antagonistic. It has to be kept in check. Alertness should never let up. As soon as there is a morally weak link in the human chain the antagonist (nuclear energy) can make use of it and endeavour to escape.

Nuclear energy is not evil. It is merely powerful. And it will not knuckle under to weak opponents.

The other aspect was presented in this way:

'One can take it that the constant radiation of nuclear waste changes the body of the earth. This negative irradiation, in the final analysis, has its place in earth history. The earth is being attacked by the germs of an illness. Up to a certain point it can absorb and digest this radiation. If this radiation exceeds a certain level, however, the earth will become seriously ill.

'What amount of renewal will take place has not yet been established. But it is the same with the world as it is with the human body when it is attacked by the germs of illness. It can cope with a certain amount, but if the level exceeds this the earth will have to go through other processes. Especially as the factors causing the earth to become sick are not restricted to nuclear waste alone but come from many other directions.

'The advancing sickness of the world runs parallel with the advancing sickness of humanity, and it is in the last resort a mirror image of humanity's situation. Nuclear waste belongs to the present earth phase. How much radiation the citizens of the earth expect to impose on their earth remains open. Human beings have their freedom!'

If we human beings would only become aware of how seriously the beings of the spiritual world take human freedom!

Why angels do not prevent evil

Again and again it happens to us human beings that when we find ourselves in an acute life situation we begin to have our doubts about a matter we were previously convinced of, and we all of a sudden no longer understand something we once thought we understood. This happened to me regarding the fact that the angels have to hold back and refrain from interfering if, out of inner freedom, human beings do not ask for help, or if it is in accordance with the destiny an individual planned before birth to go through difficult experiences. Before human beings are born on earth they are of course completely in harmony with their angels and work on their life with them. If it happens, however, that evil forces get the upper hand in us and we fall prey to them completely, resulting in terrible injustice and misery, why can our angel not step in after all to prevent worse things happening, and liberate us from the clutches of evil?

I once talked to Agnes about this. A kind of interplay arose between our conversation and the conversation with the angels. This was expressed through the words:

'When evil gets the upper hand in people they are inviting it to do so. For instance they go on thinking a bad thought until they are filled with it.

'An angel can be heard only if human beings permit it; if for example they hear in themselves a slight doubt in their bad thought and then think about whether their dark thinking is really right. Angels always want to bring light into thoughts. Human beings often hear light-filled thinking as though it were an inner voice. But they themselves have to allow the inner voice to come in. If they shut themselves off, because it is obviously much easier to choose the dark path, the angel can do nothing more. It is like wanting to burn a candle in a room where there is no oxygen. If evil gets the upper hand it draws the human being into itself. The human being is the only one who can decide who has the say, either an angel who supports the struggle to be human or a being who is antagonistic to it.'

In the course of our conversation we went on to wonder what we human beings have to do, what we have to be like, so that it is possible for angels to be active on earth. And our human conversation became a conversation with the angels again, with the words:

'Permission has to be given for angel activity. Human beings must trust them and include them in their lives. It is not always comfortable to do this. For people have constantly to hear the slight doubt in themselves. They have to be very honest with themselves. A person can ask: Was I really not to blame for the quarrel? Why do I pass on a piece of wicked gossip? The more people work on themselves the more they can work with the angels.'

Our conversation continued, and I said: All this relates to the moral weakness of individual people. Despite their conscience they give in to evil, allow it to happen. It is much more difficult when evil is absolutely not recognized and has power over people on a worldwide scale, for instance by way of the mendacity of the media, the opinion that the human being is a computer or a highly developed animal, and by way of many so-called scientific opinions that are false. We usually learn them as children in school. And what power finance and the financial world have over people! Present-day people simply grow into this spiritual void. This is what accounts for our lack of conscience towards, for example, the animal world, the earth, and particular groups of people who make a nuisance of themselves to other groups.

Every age has its own spiritual being who is there to guide humankind according to the evolutionary aims of the gods. Everyone who has spiritual vision knows that today it is the angel Michael, who ascended at the end of the nineteenth century from the rank of archangel to that of a time spirit. In the people who acknowledge him he awakens the ability to perceive the supersensible realm through the realm of the senses and to transform the human soul forces, as was described in the first part of this book. Why does Michael, the angel of our time, not bring light into souls who have been led astray? They do not even notice they are serving evil. And by and large those who do notice it do nothing about it. How are we to understand this?

First of all our attention was directed towards all that had aroused the question in me, namely that in every respect there is a noticeable weakening of human society, that a consciousness of ethical values is being lost. Yet as this is happening largely below the threshold of consciousness most people do not in the least notice it. All this is engineered by evil forces. And this flow of evil is moving darkly and sluggishly towards extinction. Those who have the will to see the light can certainly do so. All the others are being led astray without their noticing it.

After we had focused on my question once more in this form we were given a broader perspective. We were presented with a picture of the history of humankind and its laws, and we realized that throughout all the ages what has finished its development has to pass away so that something new can arise. We were told that in order to stop the persistent flow of evil something tremendous would have to happen, and that the time for this had not come yet. Evolution was not at all as hopeless as it appears to be. But it is only individuals who are receptive to the light, and not the masses. May these words encourage all those who, as individuals, for example in civil societies, speak out for change.

One more question was added here. In the book *What the Angels Need to Tell Us Now* the question of the twenty-first century was raised, and the answer was:

'Michael, the guiding angel of our time, would be only

too happy if he knew what is going to happen in the twenty-first century.'

The question that followed from this was why Michael does not know this. And we were told:

'Michael sees the paths that are open to human beings, and he sees the flow of forces and which way they are moving. But he also sees that humanity is predestined to be free. This is why, above all, he cannot or will not say what the future looks like from the spiritual perspective. Michael can of course bring the spiritual plan to realization. But as soon as human beings are included in this plan it has to be altered according to all the ways—round-about ways and mistaken ways—that human beings take. In his own sphere Michael and his angels can realize the plan of the divine ordering of the world. But on earth there are human beings who, all the time, are either moving or being moved, like the water and its tides, like the sea surging backwards and forwards, or the water in a lake stirred by the wind.'

An example of this is the question asked in another connection as to whether the prophesies had been fulfilled which Rudolf Steiner made towards the end of his life, that is, in the 1920s.* He said, for example, that towards the end of the twentieth century a number of leading anthroposophists would be on earth again. When we asked that question the angels said that Rudolf Steiner had observed correctly. In his time that had been the plan in the spiritual world. But in the further course of the century such terrible things had been committed by human beings that this plan had had to be changed. It no longer corresponded to the way the world situation had evolved up to today.

This conversation made it clear to me how consistent the

_____

*See Rudolf Steiner, *Karmic Relationships*, Vols. I to VIII, Rudolf Steiner Press.

angel world is in respecting that the predestination of humankind to have freedom is part of the divine world-plan, and how, on the other hand, an immense flexibility is being practised with regard to this plan. The most impressive thing of all, however, is the faith the world of the angels has in human beings and which is being backed up by the belief Christ has in man and also his commitment to humankind which he has brought into the world by living and dying as a human being.

We must not lose our faith in man either, despite the ever-growing power of evil in our world. For it is this faith which will open the doors to angels and enable them to be near us with their help.

The background of the many catastrophes happening today

By means of the media all the catastrophes in the world, wherever they happen, are made known worldwide. It is often said that in earlier times just as many disasters occurred but people did not hear of them so much. Yet we cannot deny the fact that since the age of modern technology there has been an increase in the number of train accidents, plane crashes, ships sinking, etc. in which a great many people lose their lives at the same time. There is also proof that natural disasters are on the increase. I am under the impression that this is telling us something, and so I asked the angels to convey to us their view on the matter.

The angels linked their reply to what they had said in the previous conversation about the dark, misdirected, sluggish-moving mire which can only be halted and made to disappear by some immense happening for which the time is not yet ripe. All the disasters happen along the path of this moving flood, as a consequence of its exudings. This mass, which is blind and rejects the realm of light, gives birth to these catastrophes. It can produce nothing else. So then I asked why these misfortunes hit so many innocent people who had often come forward to help others, and who were open to impulses of a spiritual nature, e.g. many of those who died in concentration camps? Agnes was given the answer in a picture. The dark mass is below, and further up in other regions the more light-filled souls formed other layers in the cosmos. But the disasters have such explosive force that the next layer and the one above that are also affected. The sluggish mass moves along with loud howls and the clamour is the catastrophes. It forms the path by exploding. All the people who long for light and knowledge live in another, higher sphere, not in the sluggish mass. Nevertheless they can be hit by the effects.

When such calamities happen the angels try to save people. They can draw souls out of the mass. The multitude of stories of miraculous rescues confirms this. The other light-filled souls, those who are caught up by the slimy monster, may be able to take part in the immense happening which we said is to come. For many people today the experience of so-called hell does not wait until after death, but they already go through hell on earth. This serves to awaken many sleeping souls. Although all this was a great help to me in the understanding of humanity's present situation, and why natural catastrophes often affect precisely those regions where the poor live who have been barely touched by today's negative spirit of the age, the conversation to help us understand catastrophes continued further.

We were told that the slimy masses consist of sluggish souls irrespective of which continent they live in, and what the reason for their sluggishness is: whether their thinking is over-intellectual or they do not make the effort to acquire knowledge, whether they have a cold heart or their love is animalistic, whether they exploit the earth or are indifferent to it. The catastrophes always happen where an opportunity occurs in nature or in other circumstances. The mass instigates the catastrophes, which does not mean that they happen within the mass. They also happen where the poor live. The effects are where the possibilities have provided for them. This seems at first sight to be both illogical and unjust. And yet the explosive effect of the catastrophe influences more than we see. The mass is becoming weaker in itself. It is ill, mentally and physically ill.

Do we need natural catastrophes here in Europe? Is humanity not sick in their souls here? Every country, every region has its possibility of becoming ill. A natural catastrophe seems to be a ghastly thing. Yet the way human souls are almost imperceptibly falling sick in the so-called civilized world, without anyone noticing it, and yet it affects so many people, is similar to a natural catastrophe. Every country experiences its own catastrophe, for the whole world has lost its equilibrium. I do not only accept these descriptions as information but I am living with them, thinking about them, and taking them as preparation for the 'immense happening' which is the sole remedy for the salvation of catastrophe-ridden human beings.

Abortion

In my profession as a priest I am continually encountering the emotional distress of women who have had an abortion. A lot of them try to live with this fact, but some of them carry it along as a heavy burden until shortly before their death or beyond. Many of them seek advice before going through with it. I do not remove the decision from them, for after all they have to live with the consequences, and they will be able to go forward only on the basis of their own independent resolve and not on an outside opinion. But I offer to give them practical help if they have the child, and I have in many cases done so. It is wonderful to see what strong souls arrive on earth as a result of a resolve that has had to be fought for like this. And it is sad to see how souls suffer when they find that they are not wanted. I have even seen a few examples of children who felt their foster or adoptive parents to be their true parents. For instance, on beginning at school a little girl told me that her angel was not paying attention and sent her at first to the wrong mother. When he noticed the mistake he saw to it that she reached her right mother. This child spent the first weeks of her life in a babys' home and she screamed when anyone tried to touch her. When a friend of a nurse at the home came on a visit she asked to help feed the children. As she approached this little one's cot the baby held out her arms to her, beamed at her and let her give her the bottle without any trouble. The woman felt immediately what the child was trying to tell her, and she succeeded in adopting her. Another three-year old told his mother: 'I tried to come to you three times, but you always shut the door.'

How women and children deal with an abortion varies to a tremendous extent. When I once asked the angels for their perception I was told the following:

'A number of the souls know in advance that they will be aborted. They choose their parents according to their karma a long time before their conception, as is the case with every other child. It is only that they know that they have no or very little chance of seeing the light of day and incarnating. Their period of incarnation in the maternal body is just a few weeks. They have then fulfilled their and their parents' karma. They had only a very small circle to describe on earth, and they managed to do that. These are often souls who are attached to their mother – or parents – with strong bonds of love, and take this path upon themselves for this reason. Their rapid departure is usually known to them beforehand. They can see that their parents do not want to accept them by their vibrations, their spiritual colours. They often exert a strong influence on their parents' lives without ever being born. They have a lasting effect on their parents' destiny. These souls have a very short journey after death. They and all the spiritual beings connected to this destiny help look for a couple who will accept their arrival.

'It is far more difficult for souls where no definite decision has been made to have an abortion. A tremendous amount of pain comes to the unborn soul from such abortions. For they have been preparing their incarnation together with their angel over a long period of time, have co-ordinated their plans with the angels of the people with whom they are karmically connected, and with whom they have some imbalance to redress from a previous life, or to take something further or to endeavour to begin something new. They are now prevented from being able to realize this life plan on earth. The child's karma is struck by a huge wave of disappointment and sadness. These souls need much longer to recover from the disappointment over their short span of life in their mother's body for it does not tally with the course of life they had prepared. A soul of this kind will also find replacement parents, but it will take a much longer time.

'It may seem surprising that there are two different procedures in this area. It makes a tremendous difference, however, for the souls who are coming, whether they know what awaits them or whether it happens to them unexpectedly.

'The souls who know beforehand devote themselves lovingly to the two people in the position of parents who have to carry the karmic consequences of preventing a human being from entering earth life. This now belongs to their lives and they have to mature through it, and the rejected soul is willing to give them support. Therefore these parents have particular reason to concern themselves with what happened because of them and take it as a challenge to undergo inner development. They also, of course, have new karmic responsibilities towards the rejected soul and its destiny. The souls who do not know in advance that they are going to be prevented from incarnating, and the parents who do not know initially what they will decide, run into tremendous emotional strain and mental distress. These children have a much more difficult and painful struggle to redress the balance.'

There is a great danger involved here, namely that people might relate this description too quickly to their own plight. They could take this as an excuse and say that this soul whose incarnation they have prevented knew of it and did not want it to happen differently. This description must under no circumstances be misused. There are other possible karmic paths to take, where every human endeavour must be made to pursue what has been started in a worthy and humanly appropriate way. For example in the case of a marriage crisis there must not be a natural assumption that the karma between the two of them is finished and a new one can begin with someone else. Crises always indicate that something has not been mastered. But it may be the case that the people concerned are too weak to cope with the crisis and that the situation makes things especially difficult. Perhaps it compares with being in traffic. A driver has to do everything he can to avoid an accident. Wear a safety-belt, not drive too close to the vehicle in front, take no risks overtaking, etc. If there is nevertheless an accident we can only talk of destiny if everything humanly possible has been done to avoid one. We cannot simply say that everything is due to destiny, whether we behave properly or not. It is the same with a decision to have an abortion as it is with human relations. Here too you must be aware that through such decisions new karma will arise.

Perhaps it would be a good thing at this juncture to elucidate the concept of karma. It is taken for granted here that human beings live on earth not only once but that in accordance with their development along the path to full humanhood and the fulfilment of the task given to humanity as a whole to carry out the words of creation 'Created in the image of God', we incarnate again and again to undergo experiences only possible on earth. We therefore bring with us things connecting us to other people which require taking further and being redressed and made good again. This is past karma, which has to occur in some way as it is subject to spiritual necessity. However, there is also future karma, and this has its origin in the present life, arising out of the possibility of doing something in freedom. But unfree deeds also have consequences in the future. 'Karma' is the old term used to designate these involvements and effects passing from one life to another.

The population explosion

We repeatedly encounter the view that overpopulation on earth is the cause of many problems and catastrophes. This is pursued to the point where people want to establish a law, as they have already in China, to forbid a family to have more than one or two children.

The angels see this quite differently:

'There is no such thing as a population explosion. Only more people or fewer people on earth. For what appears to be too many only appears so at first sight. It will happen of itself that humankind decimates itself. At present there is an imbalance among the various peoples, but karma will bring it about that it becomes evened out.'

Sudden death

When the death of a loved one occurs suddenly by way of an accident or a very short illness we human beings are overwhelmed, and we lack the understanding and often the strength too, to work through such an occurrence. In this chapter, in which the angels express themselves on this subject, they put themselves entirely into the position of us human beings and use the term 'we'.

'Sudden death takes a person away from us and leaves a vacuum. We handle this vacuum in the way we mourn. We can either stretch this vacuum into an eternity and disappear in it ourselves, or we can endeavour to let it remain at a "normal" length and fill it with light so as to bring about transformation.

'A sudden death leaves a gap behind, and all kinds of fears, longings, and also demands on the deceased one for love, protection etc. flow into this gap. If this gap gets too big it devours us.

'When a person close to us is taken from us we suddenly lose our balance. Our capacity to feel at home in our surroundings is reduced. We have to learn afresh how to fit in. This also gives us the chance to make a totally new start. There is perhaps not only a gap left behind, for we may also notice how much the departed one set their mould on us. We can ask ourselves whether we are really like this, or did we just adapt to it? We get the chance to change our lives altogether. An important element that had settled in at our side was removed. Now we can thread the chain differently and decide ourselves whether this element is going to be replaced or how we can shape the new chain.

'Death reminds us that we are all only temporary guests on earth. In the case of a slow death no such vacuum arises, because for a long time the patient has been getting weaker and weaker. A violent death has something about it that tears at us, and we feel this at the person's departure. The harsh effect on us puts us in a panic, fills us with fear. The vacuum left behind is very compact and is not so easily defused. It takes longer to work through this sort of vacuum. A violent death never happens by chance, how-ever. Karma is often making its appearance here. And always redressing something, never uncalled for.

'When sudden death occurs a person's spiritual part no longer has a body. The people on earth can do a great deal for the deceased; they ought to make contact with the departed one spiritually, because during the first few days after death it is still just wandering around. They should beg the soul to let go of the earth, and explain why it should do so. The deceased's next of kin should also let it go. Through prayer one can also ask the higher worlds for help.'

Let me describe an incident that supports this. Many years ago there was a plane crash in Switzerland in which many people experienced sudden death. An anthro-posophical doctor, who had devoted a lot of thought to life after death, died around the same time. While the priest was performing her funeral service in the crematorium he experienced that the whole hall was filled with the souls of the crash victims. In an inner gesture he spoke the words for all of them. Then it appeared to him as if the doctor took the lead and helped all those souls to find their way into the realm of the afterlife.

Another question relating to violent death was whether a murder can be karmically intended? Whether a murderer *has* to commit the murder. Surely this produces new karmic obligation for the next incarnation? The response was:

'If a person is destined to depart from earthly life prematurely there are various possibilities: accidents, strokes and other things. Another possibility is murder. This theme is very complex and is different from case to case. The murderer does not have to commit the murder in order to balance karma. That would be the very worst possibility. What was determined was that the deceased should depart this life at a definite point in time. Various possibilities exist, however. There could possibly also be a tragedy occurring between two people in this life which leads to a murder. The murderer obviously brings a new karmic debt upon himself. Although there are other terrible things that serve to bring about balance, such as tormenting someone (psycho-terror, as it is called nowadays).'

And what is happening in the case of mass murders? 'These deaths, resulting from arbitrary human decision, are not so arbitrary. The murderer is usually no longer his own master. He is possessed and is being used. The victims were lined up around him beforehand, as in a spider's web. Who lines the victims up? It is a karmic arrangement. Yet tremendous imbalance arises, the redressing of which will call for a great deal of strength.'

I asked about the millions of children who die annually of hunger. 'These souls who are deprived of the bodily foundation to survive become more spiritual. The bodily need for food becomes too great. Then, after a certain stage, it becomes very small, and a spiritual power, surpassing the human spirit, increases. These souls are performing a sacrifice for humanity.'

What of the children who die through ill-treatment? 'This theme, too, should be looked at very individually. These children also are making a kind of sacrifice which they already decided upon before birth. Right from the beginning they chose a path of destiny which will bring much agony and which will give them a very slender chance of survival. They do in fact perform a sacrifice through which they ascend even higher.'

Again and again I became pre-occupied with the question of how the spiritual world looked at and judged suicide. I had been asked a number of times in my life to perform a funeral service for suicides who had been refused a Christian burial by other churches. I had the feeling that these people were in special need of Christian help. In one case the bereaved wife had a kind of dream in which she saw the husband hovering round a house in despair because the doors and windows were securely locked and he could find no way in. This is an image of the fact that people who have taken their own lives often regret it immediately afterwards and want to get back into their body. It is terrible for them that this is no longer possible. But this wife had already had the impression when they got married that her husband would not grow old. Through experiences of this kind and many others I arrived at the question of whether there is such a thing as justified suicide sanctioned by karma, by God? I found the answer very helpful:

'Yes, there is. Particularly nowadays there are lives which were over earlier, yet are artifically prolonged through medicine. Then it is justified for a patient to refuse everything that would contribute to an artificial lengthening of life. The patients decide themselves that they will die. This must be distinguished from suicide.' (This does not mean what nowadays we call assisted suicide, but a natural death which is not prolonged by artificial means.) 'Fundamentally there is no karmic necessity. The pain process should be borne as far as it is acceptable. In the case of people who are being kept alive solely by artificial means it is more a learning process for the relatives. In the case of a suicide due to debts, jealousy or apparent hopelessness, the angels will always try to restrain the person. Where psychological illnesses are concerned it varies considerably. With such conditions people are not in control. Basically it holds good that a person may not choose suicide to escape from an unpleasant, difficult period of life. If people defraud themselves of a part of their lives, that is not karmically determined. We are full of mercy!'

With this last statement the angels probably want to tell us that we human beings do not have the right to condemn suicides or actually to deny them a Christian burial. They of all people have need of our helping prayers!

I would like at this juncture to mention another incident. Many years ago a young man in our community took his own life. He had spent a term at a priest seminar after which he made use of his training as a teacher and took a post in higher education. He had no difficulties in his profession and was happily engaged. One evening, whilst in the school laboratory, he observed a snake shedding its skin. The following day his colleagues found a short note from him left near the snake, telling them that just as the snake shed its skin he wanted to discard his human skin and live a new life. Forty days later they found his body in the woods under the snow. An old priest who, ever since his own son fell to his death in the mountains, had had the ability to perceive departed souls, was asked by the young man's mother-in-law whether he could tell her how her son-in-law fared. To his own surprise the priest was shown that the young man was not a human being at all but an angel. The mother-in-law too was amazed, and recalled that at the priest seminar the young man had taken the lead in a dramatized version of Leo Tolstoi's story 'What men live by'. It is about a shoemaker who, on his way home, finds a naked man leaning against the wall of a chapel. He gives him his coat, takes him along with him and makes him his apprentice. He experiences unusual things with him, for the young man knows more about his customers than he does himself. It is finally revealed that he is an angel who had a certain task to fulfil on earth, and he then takes his leave of the earth and of his human form.

Decades later I now asked the angels whether this sort of thing really happens and whether it actually applied in the case cited above. They confirmed this but warned against speculating with such thoughts.

Death by cyanide

Many people who know the lecture Rudolf Steiner gave about cyanide* for the workers at the Goetheanum are concerned and depressed about the problem he spoke of there. A doctor has given the following report on it.

'I had the opportunity to hear from behind a wall a lecture Rudolf Steiner gave to the workers in the carpenters' shop. In this lecture Rudolf Steiner mentioned that in a case of cyanide poisoning a human being's soul was destroyed to the point of not being able to move on a straight path to the sun sphere but only by way of many diverse routes. As I could not imagine that a physical substance of material

---

* See *Mensch und Welt, Das Wirken des Geistes in der Natur* (GA 351), lecture of 10 October 1923.

origin could have such an effect on the soul that it would still be under its influence after death, I asked Rudolf Steiner about this. He was prepared straight away to explain it to me, and said roughly the following:

' "A human being's etheric body [the organization of our life forces. I.J.] is bound to the physical body by oxygen. The moment cyanide gets into the body the oxygen is changed into nitrogen. This breaks up the etheric body so that after death people do not see the review of their lives. [Everything people experience imprints itself in the course of earthly life into their etheric body. After death we look back at this panorama imprinted on our etheric body. I.J.] The hierarchies of the angels, however, concern themselves with saving human souls, but it is a gruesome task for them. People such as this return to the world in their next incarnation as cripples, and this can only be redressed over several incarnations.

'To my question as to whether cyanide would be used in the next war he said "No", but that other terrible things were in the pipeline. When I asked him whether these would come about in America, he said: "No, in Germany." '*

We now know that in concentration camps people were put to death by cyanide gas in their millions, and many are concerned to know whether, despite their innocence, they will have to go through this terrible after-death existence and the consequences that follow in further incarnations. In my case too, this question kept on recurring. So I asked the angels to tell me about it. And I was told:

'This process and the effects cyanide has on the etheric body still exists today. But where those who died in the holocaust are concerned the following happened. Their

*P. Selg, *Antroposophische Ärzte*, Verlag am Goetheanum.

etheric bodies were certainly torn to pieces. But by virtue of the other conditions these were immediately restored. There is a difference between a mass murder of hundreds of thousands of innocents and one person's suicide. These souls do not need to be born as cripples either. Why should they have to bear this fate as well? When suicide is committed by means of cyanide the soul was already torn to bits. That is why these people choose this method of killing themselves.

'When criminals in the USA are condemned to die in this way, what happens in the afterlife is a very individual matter. Through very hard work on the part of the angels these human souls can be saved. It depends on what the person was like on earth. In the case of criminals who already in this life are trying to dissolve themselves, it is a self-chosen destiny to die of cyanide poisoning. So it can well be their karma to be executed in this way. Otherwise the angels do all in their power to save the person's after-life.'

Aids

If you have ever had anything to do with someone suffering from Aids you will certainly be keen to know what this illness has to tell us. The answer I received gave me even more to think about.

'Aids is an unusual illness. Even the means of transmitting it, which happens almost totally by means of sexual intercourse and the blood, distinguishes it from other illnesses. It is an infectious disease, and yet it works in quite a different way from epidemics of the past. Aids bears the sign of the Cross. Those affected by it go the way of the Cross, as Jesus did. Yet they do not take the Cross upon themselves, they do not carry it, but they move along the Cross which is their path. They stand out from the crowd. They die for other people. They take upon themselves the guilt of others. They die for humankind. They themselves are not guilty. They should not be condemned. They bear the guilt of humankind. The illness is like an abyss of fire. There are many stones, but a few of them become like magma, volcanic rock which melts and falls into the gorge. Those who believe they can make judgements are imprisoned in themselves.

'Through the fact that this disease can be passed on only through bodily fluids one can see how relevant to our times it is. It affects the person's innermost being. It does not allow of any choice. There is no cure. At the end of the way is death. This illness has its place in our times and shows where humanity stands today. What a good thing that there are people who take this difficult path.'

For angels everything is good that is spiritually true and is in tune with them.

I asked further what exactly was meant by this illness belonging to our times. And I was told:

'Because it is only in the present time that this illness is possible in this form. At this time the forces of the living organism are being so misused, treated through human choice and egotism with such disdain and ignorance, that this affects the bodily carrier of these life forces, the fluids of the blood and of sex. It also brings home to the scientists who consider themselves all-mighty the limits of their possibilities. The Aids victims are sacrificing their own lives to compensate for the misuse of life among present-day humanity. They resolved to do this voluntarily before their birth, apart from the few who were mentioned earlier in connection with the picture of the magma.'

The brutalizing of sexuality

Whilst presenting the background behind Aids mention has of course already been made of the misuse and the coarsening of the life forces of sexuality today. In answer to our question as to whether there was a connection between the coarsening of sexuality and the decrease in the power of people's immune system, their susceptibility to infection and disease, we were told:

'Consciously or unconsciously human beings are exposing themselves to very bad influences. They take not the slightest care of their aura, of their inner harmony. They do not cultivate their spiritual part. They are becoming impoverished. With so many weak human beings the whole of the earth's living space is out of balance. This is the soil in which disease and infection breed. The many weak people "pollute" the living space. Everybody who spends time on earth is hit by it. One cannot escape the present life. One of the causes of this is the coarsening of sexuality. This works in exactly the same way on the harmony of the earth's living space. It weakens it. Human beings do not realize how much of their ego is being torn out of them by cohabitation of such a kind.'

Here too I had to think of the description Rudolf Steiner gave of the evil powers who set themselves in the place of the true being of love, the Christ, namely the Antichrist, the evil beings belonging to him, and the asuras. One of the active areas in which they tear away pieces of a human beings' ego is the misuse, the coarsening of sexuality.*

Battles between spiritual beings are actually concealed behind all these present-day circumstances, all these problems, aberrations and abuses of present-day humanity.

---

*See Rudolf Steiner, *The Deed of Christ*, Steiner Book Centre, 1976.

Those in the service of humanity's progressive evolution battle against those who mean to prevent it. This is why we human beings need to ally ourselves with those beings who are willing to help us, choosing freedom to include them in our lives.

The senses and the soul as organs of perception for the spiritual in nature

Over many years I have been constantly endeavouring to observe nature in the way that was pioneered by Goethe and which I have described to some extent in the chapter on creative thinking. Goethe looked at the individual parts of a plant: the root, sprout, stem, leaf, bud, blossom, stamen, fruit and seed not as a series of component parts, but as an inner process leading one form over into the next one, each in its own way. He called this process the 'metamorphosis of the plant'. By making an exact observation of the plant and reproducing it in thought a human being gets to know its being. The idea of the plant takes on form within him.

I once attended a course in which we were given exercises to help us to transform our souls into organs of perception with which we can learn to experience spiritual beings in nature. It struck me that this was quite a different process from the one I had been practising for decades. The course also began with a description of a plant as presented to us by our senses. Then we were asked to observe the plant not only from outside but to perceive it with our feeling. This gave us the impression that in making this approach to it we were robbing it of some of its life forces. So we poured out our whole love towards this plant whose evolutionary stages we had got to know. And it seemed as though the plant recovered again, as you can experience on the physical plane when a drooping plant straightens up when it is watered.

There awoke in me the question as to what actually happens if we encounter a plant in Goethe's way or feel our way into it with love? What role does Goetheanism play in the endeavour to include the spiritual world in nature? I was given a new way of looking at this question:

'You open your soul to the spirit in nature if you feel your way into the being of the plant by trying for example to observe the different stages of a plant over the course of a year. With this method of Goethe's you get in touch with these processes and make yourself open for spiritual perceptions which have to do with the plant. If you now proceed to observe your own soul and sense what the soul is making of its observation of the plant, then a dialogue comes about, i.e. an exchange between the plant and the human being ensues: a vibration from the human being to the plant and the plant to the human being. In Goetheanism the vibration passes from the plant to the person but not in the form of a dialogue, not the other way round. Only with certain people did Goetheanism become a dialogue, as these people were able to perceive the plant with their hearts. Goetheanism is the first step towards communicating with a plant. Soul language is the second step. Today it is possible to pass over the first step and start straight away with the second. A short while ago the time had not come for it. People were not ready for it.'

I asked whether one would be able to perceive the being of a tree or elemental beings just as well with closed eyes, and the answer was:

'Anyone who can see the being of a tree with their eyes open can also sense it with closed eyes, and vice versa. Someone who cannot see them with their eyes open does not see them with closed eyes either. Some people have their perceptions very differently. For instance they can concentrate better with their eyes closed. But the above-mentioned rule applies on the whole. It is right for a person to aim predominantly for inner perception, for this should be the way of seeing of the future.'

Later I read the following paragraph by Andreas Heertsch in a periodical: 'I have the hope that in our scientific work we are facing a change of paradigm which will extend the necessary era of Goetheanism into the realm of anthroposophical science, i.e. that it will go beyond the interpreting of or giving of a new interpretation to existing phenomena, and by means of symbolizing and meditation will approach the etheric world from inside.'*

This spurred me on to ask one more question on this subject, namely whether Goetheanism can also be a hindrance. I was told: 'No, everyone has to find the path that suits them.'

Are children more difficult nowadays than they used to be?

One is perpetually coming across differences of opinion from parents and teachers. Some say that the inner laws which Rudolf Steiner specified at the beginning of the twentieth century as applying to growing children no longer apply today. Therefore we should not teach according to these but according to developmental laws which have undergone change in the course of time. Otherwise children will become more and more difficult. Others think that it is not the developmental pattern of children and young people which is changing but that this

*See *Das Goetheanum*, Dornach 47/2000.

is being given different forms and means of expression by all the influences coming from the environment. I asked the angels for their view of this problem and received the following answer:

'The developmental laws which apply to children today are the same as they were at the beginning of the twentieth century. But souls go through a different "light colour", of course, when they come now at the beginning of the twenty-first century. What we mean by "colour of light" are the different, variable relationships between the cosmos and the earth which certain people choose because they suit their destiny and plans. Therefore the demands made on children today are quite different now. These souls no longer have the prescribed limits which used to apply. (Family, authority, society...). People live much more as individuals today. Children are made insecure by the sheer proliferation of choice. They are not more difficult than they were a hundred years ago, just less secure.

'The demands made on them are also much greater. Children in the past certainly had to go out to work earlier and carry responsibility, whereas today they are often left to their own devices and have to decide for themselves what is good for them. The things that create difficulties for teachers nowadays, e.g. that children are hyperactive, disrespectful, brutal, egoistic and precocious, can have very different causes. There are hyperactive children who have brought this tendency with them but because of their "good environment" do not bring it to expression. There are hyperactive children who, because they are born into a family in crisis, struggle throughout their lives with the inclination to be constantly pulled in all directions.

'Children do not bring more difficulties with them than they used to. It is just that their karmically-based difficulties fall into better soil and develop much faster and more intensely than before (almost artificially fast—just as everything at the present time is speeding up). To be disrespectful, inconsiderate and egoistic is of course inherent in the child's own being, but these traits depend very much on how the child is handled. Children who are cruel are often tormented souls. The cause of this does not necessarily lie in present but in past happenings. It is such a pity that these souls find no other way, or rather they are not shown another way of freeing themselves from this.

'The children who are coming now have to make a strong bond with the earth yet at the same time be very open to higher things. This calls for a tremendous struggle for balance.

'Souls are more delicate and vulnerable. This is why they often make themselves so unresponsive, so that they cannot be hurt so badly. But this "sensitivity" is very important today.'

There are teachers and publications today that are fully in agreement with the way the angels see this. For example see descriptions of so-called 'indigo children' in popular literature.

Andy Warhol

I saw an exhibition of pictures by Andy Warhol. There were numerous examples of the way he has altered Leonardo da Vinci's picture of 'The Last Supper', 'modernized' it, transposed it into our time. Anyone who loves Leonardo's picture certainly finds this hard to stomach. I wanted to know how such a phenomenon is judged from a higher point of view. What I was told opened up a totally new view:

'Nothing is rigid. Everything changes. That picture is

unique – but does that make it inviolable? Every individual comes to grips with God in one way or another. People grapple with this. It is of interest to an artist to alter that unique picture, to enable it to become part of himself. To play with it, to be able to make something of it. The artist wanted to pull it down from its pedestal. Wanted to turn it into common property. He has done it with a lot of love. He was searching for God – but was he aware of this? It was an approach. Andy Warhol did not just come upon this picture by chance. He came to grips with it. Possibly even made fun of it. But he nevertheless considered it as "sacred".'

This modernization of Leonardo's 'Last Supper' had seemed to me to be a gross violation of that great work. I only gradually came to understand that the angels do not see this picture as an artistic product but see what takes place in the artist himself as he paints it, and that this is somewhat different in the twentieth century from how it was in earlier centuries. They acknowledge and love a human being who is genuinely striving and they do not compare one work of art with another. They understand the people of our time much better than many of us do.

Psychological and existential welfare

Nowadays there are innumerable methods of helping people who have psychological problems. There are the various forms of psychotherapy, e.g. gestalt therapy, communication therapy, art therapy, FamilyConstellation and biography work. All those who have acquired experience of their own in this area are free to take from the words of the angels what applies to themselves and their encounters. It has often happened to me that people come to me because they could not cope with the experiences they met with in the course of psychotherapy or biography seminars. They were often compelled to remain totally occupied with themselves.

As a start I was first given aspects that applied in general to this whole complex of problems:

'There are many ways of getting to know a person's problems. In many instances an attentive listener is all that is required so that the person has the chance to get things off their chest. Some problems lie considerably deeper, i.e. the problems are brought from a previous life. The conflicts somebody now has with certain people are conflicts from earlier times. As long as psychotherapy does not take karma into account it will not find definite solutions.

'If this biography work is looked at as a small part of a large chain, and this life is the latest link so to speak, then it can be thoroughly positive. However, if this last link is twisted and turned until it is worn through, and the connection with other links is no longer recognizable, this work can not be seen as positive.'

This was followed by a picture which helped me very much to understand the problems:

'The human being is like a pearl. The innermost part of the pearl is the soul. Psychotherapy and biography work look chiefly at the newest layer on the outside (childhood, youth . . .). And people think that if they throw enough light on it, this is "knowing themselves". But that is like shovelling snow. When you have shovelled away the newly fallen snow you reach a sheet of ice. This sheet of ice is far more difficult to work with. But the sheet of ice is the actual problem.

'Some of the work in psychology respects karmic connections but pays very little attention to them. As it is considerably more difficult to work on the ice which is barely penetrable, people are proud enough of being able to shovel snow. In our opinion one should not even need to shovel the snow. When the moment of "awakening" has come the inner sun will penetrate both the snow and the ice.'

I once asked whether it could be beneficial in the course of therapy to bring it about that people consciously encounter themselves, that is, through another person. The answer was:

'Everyone, particularly nowadays, has the unconscious desire to encounter themselves. To grasp the meaning of their existence. But as people can often no longer accept Christ they can also not recognize their life's destiny. In their search for help they turn to therapists.

'If this experience is induced – and people are usually not ready for it – they cannot cope with it. It can even happen that greater damage is done, or the whole thing can have no sense. If people do not feel the love of Christ they will not be supported in their agony. This is not a healthy method. A wound is torn open and no-one attends to it. This experience can only be borne with the spiritual support and the power and help of Christ.

'The sacrament centering the ego, as is practised in the Christian Community, helps people to realize where they are in their biography, and they become ready, with the help and power of Christ, to accept the consequences of their deeds, thoughts and feelings.'

Fear and its effect

I keep pondering the phenomenon of fear. How much of what we do is done out of fear! We pay for expensive insurance cover for fear of theft, fire and accident, etc. People are afraid of commitments because they do not know beforehand how things will turn out. They are afraid of illnesses, of the possibility of having a retarded child, preferring to cope instead with medical experts, a course which involves tremendous disadvantages and dangers of a different kind.

Nuclear rearmament was pursued out of fear of another war and the defeat of their own people. You can go on forever. Fear is soil for further fears. Yet in many situations it is just a signal, a warning of danger. Feeling the need to do justice to this fear which appears as so negative, I asked the angels about the nature of fear. I received a broad answer.

'Fear attacks people from behind and gets them in its grip. Fear warns people not to carry out ill-considered actions. Fear fills people's auras with a different light, one that electrifies them. This tension can be both positive and negative. Fear is human. The kind of fear which comes not from instinct but from reason is a worthy quality. Fear is a valuable asset.'

I was reminded that Christ did not say to his disciples: 'You do not need to be afraid, I have overcome fear for you,' but rather: 'Fear is of the world. But be comforted, I have overcome the world.' So the important thing is to put fear in its right place.

Religious services for the young

Probably ministers of every Christian denomination are concerned about the problem of what they can do so that more young people will come to their services. Some of them try jazz and pop music, or having religious festivals run by the young people themselves, or giving sermons in the 'cool' language of youth. As far as I am concerned the ritual of the mass in the Christian Community is not a human invention but given for our time from out of Christ's world, therefore it cannot be altered according to our own discretion. So the question arose in me whether for young people after their confirmation, i.e. from the age of 14–18, they ought to have their own form of religious service, because it is difficult for them to listen for long without saying anything themselves or fidgeting. The answer was:

'No, this is not the case. The course of the service is exactly right. Whether people are young or old, everybody needs the calm emanating from the ritual to attune themselves to the sacrament. Impatient people, those in a hurry, find it difficult to calm down at first, of course. People have to find their own approach to the service from out of their own destiny. Many only begin looking for it when they are hit by adversity and are looking for answers. The young will have already absorbed the image of Christ in their religious lessons. However, during adolescence young people question everything, including everything they have heard about Christ. When they are a bit older, the fundamentals that have formed the basis for their inner being start to be active in their hearts. And in due course it will occur to them that there is a community which they could also become part of. The need to turn to Christ can often only arise in a person's own self. The giving of oneself can only happen when a person's heart is open. The language of the ritual is in tune with this.'

Ecumenical matters

I once conducted a funeral for a young man in conjunction with a Catholic priest. The deceased had been christened and confirmed in the Christian Community, had been to the Steiner Waldorf School, and was also a child of his village in which he had grown up and where everyone was fond of him. The village population was Catholic. The Catholic burial service is preceded by mass, and this was held by the Catholic priest. It took place in the baroque village church. I took part in my Christian Community vestments, gave the address during the mass and then the blessing and the burial at the grave according to the ritual of the Christian Community. The congregation were very impressed by this ecumenical service, and the Catholic priest particularly so.

Since then I have been left with the question as to whether sacraments carried out in an ecumenical way are meaningful. For example I have always declined to celebrate an ecumenical wedding ceremony. When I asked for a higher viewpoint I received the following answer:

'Yes, the churches should unite, but in a spiritual way, not in the way services are celebrated today! If a wedding ceremony is celebrated by a Protestant and a Catholic priest a confusion arises. What is intended to be progressive and liberating has been wrongly understood. Is it expecting too much that people could decide either to have a Catholic wedding or a Protestant one? Most people are not so religious, all they want is a solemn framework for their celebrations. It is like a mixture of black and white. Both are absolutely pure colours. But when you mix them you get grey, which is formless. Everyone can discover for themselves what form or mixture they are choosing. But a jumble is what they will be left with if in their wedding arrangements they cannot come to terms with their faith. On the face of it there seems nothing wrong with choosing both.

'From a spiritual point of view the churches ought to be on friendly terms, for after all they have the same Saviour. But what do people achieve by mixing things? There is the possibility of choice, but they tinker with everything, so as not to have to stand by their faith, not to have to decide or even take time to think. These people imagine they are unconventional and free. Though actually they cannot just let "anything go" by choosing to do things differently. Only when people are indifferent about what happens on the spiritual level is it done this way. The correct thing to do would be for each of them to maintain their own direction and for them to have mutual recognition of the fact. If people tackle the question of faith seriously they must eventually come to a decision. Until they have decided, of course, they are not committed. But one ought to have a goal in sight.'

Democracy and the threefold social order

For more than eighty years pupils of Rudolf Steiner have been working with the idea of the threefold social order which he wanted to bring to the attention of those in power in Germany at the end of the First World War in the hope that it would come to realization.* But the attempt was not successful. Then a number of business concerns endeavoured to bring elements of it into practice, e.g. the German pharmaceutical firm Wala and the community hospital at Herdecke. The Central European GLS bank is likewise aimed at realizing this idea. Yet despite many small endeavours people failed to launch the idea either in Germany or Europe or even America. It was accepted nowhere, neither among the ruling powers nor among the people. A few people still work on the idea, and there are still attempts here and there to put it into practice. But many of those who have promoted it have meanwhile gained the impression that it is still too early for it.

---

*See Rudolf Steiner, *Towards Social Renewal*, Rudolf Steiner Press, 1999.

I wondered how present political, economic and cultural conditions in the so-called western world are regarded by the spiritual world. I asked the angels whether the democratic form of government was right for humankind today or which quite new form it should take? The answer was a definite 'No' to democracy. All forms of government, whether democracy, a republic, bolshevism or the aristocracy are as good or as bad as any other. It does not matter which is in power. For in all of these the politicians are no better than the citizens. It would require a high level of morality to introduce a new form of government, and there is a great scarcity of this at the moment. Any form of government with a high level of ethics would be preferable to all the forms existing today. But nothing will appear unless it comes from people at grass roots level. The present democratic form of government is supported by a great many pillars. These are the various vested interests. Some of the pillars are very strong, whereas others are about to collapse. From a spiritual point of view there is no balance, no question of equal rights for all citizens. The work Nicanor Perlas is doing with his friends is very important for the future.*

Agnes sees this in a picture. There is a floating island, and Nicanor is driving buttresses into it to support it. The people who want to support his work are gathering around these supportive buttresses. But from time to time there are lots of trouble-makers who want to hamper anything new that has to come about. The time will come when the whole island will be turned around. Then the disrupters will disappear. Things have not reached that point yet, but the work people are doing round Nicanor

---

* See Nicanor Perlas, *Shaping Globalization: Civil Society, Cultural Power and Threefolding*, Global Net 3, 2000.

Perlas is helping to prepare for it. It is by no means in vain.

The transformation of evil into a higher good

When, after the end of the Second World War, what had been happening in the concentration camps of the Hitler regime became more and more widely known, and we became aware of the consummate skill with which the mass murders had been accomplished, I could hardly bear these impressions, and I actually avoided coming to terms with these facts. Then one day the book by Jesaiah Ben-Aharon came into my hands, *The Spiritual Event of the Twentieth Century, An Imagination**. He describes a spiritual event which he himself experienced as one born after those events. Having been born in Israel, and not having had anything to do with Christianity, he saw Christ descending from the spiritual world into the deepest evil of humanity in order to transform it into a higher good. He saw that the prayers of love and intercession which had been offered by Christians for 2000 years were being concentrated and gathered together by a group of human beings in the period between their previous death on earth and a new birth, and who were preparing for their earthly life as pupils of the leading time spirit, Michael. These human beings were gathering together the Christianized forces of love and forming them into a kind of spiritual heart organ, the spiritual heart of a future humanity. And out of this heart they were sending down streams of love, of comfort and of strength to the people who were being tormented, tortured and totally destroyed. That streaming love bore Christ

---

* Temple Lodge Publishing, 2nd edition, 1996.

down into the depths of evil to transform it. The book woke me from the nightmare which the horrors of the Third Reich had signified for me.

Already in his time Rudolf Steiner cautiously intimated that Christ would accomplish a second great deed of sacrifice. Just as he had wrested the resurrection from death, he would wrest from evil a higher good for the salvation of humankind. This was what would enable human beings to experience the reappearance of Christ. Since hearing those announcements telling us of events in the spiritual world I looked for happenings on earth in which I could recognize the effects of these events. I imagined I could see signs of them in the moving accounts of prisoners who even in their lifetime were capable of forgiving their tormenters. A book bearing the title *Stimme des Menschen* ('Human Voices') containing the last words, letters and records of condemned prisoners, had an introduction consisting of a prayer by a Jewish person imploring help for the murderers after their death.

Time and again I encountered examples such as these, and I wondered whether this was what was meant by the transformation of evil into a higher good. For this kind of forgiveness and this pleading on behalf of the most inhuman of criminals is more than a human being can achieve alone. That is a higher good in him, it is Christ in him. But I found I had to understand in another way also the Imagination Ben Aharon described, namely that not only is a higher good awakened through the sacrifice offered on behalf of the evil of slaughtering so many people, but that the evil in the perpetrators themselves is transformed.

I asked Agnes to elucidate this question for me with the help of the angels. This is how the conversation arose in which my question was considered from several aspects.

The first thing we were told was that when people are really evil, such as the camp guards were, they are no longer their own master. Evil beings hold them captive. When Christ descends into such people he digs deeper and deeper until he finds their soul, which is like a pearl. He then takes this 'spiritual' soul and leads it to the light. Agnes asked: 'Where is this soul when the person dies?'

It was explained to us that the true ego-soul is with Christ and that only the 'shadow-soul' remains in the human being. At death the shadow-soul departs from the body and seeks its ego-soul. The angels put it into Agnes' language and called it the 'original soul'. In this process the shadow-soul is not lost, for it seeks its true self in the light.

With regard to my need to be able to imagine everything as concretely as possible, or to recognize it again here in life, I was told that as an earthly human being one cannot experience this concretely and create it afresh, because it is not externally visible. The description continued: 'This act of Christ digging to find the soul which is buried alive is very strenuous and actually dangerous.' Agnes saw a picture of being inside a dark mountain, digging and digging, looking for a minute light which can actually not remain alive any longer down there in the dark.

Agnes then asked my actual question: 'Does Christ do that by himself descending into the evil people whilst they are doing evil?' And before she continued speaking she received an emphatic: 'Yes.' Then she went on to ask: 'Or does he do that in the person who is the victim of other people's evil?' We were told:

'Sacrifices made through great goodness and moral power for the sake of forgiving the perpetrator have a connection with the perpetrators whose souls are being transformed. When the Christ enters the perpetrators to bring their souls to the light this original, true soul light, which is Christ in them, shines on the victims. Through the power of Christ which is being activated, they can develop their own goodness and moral power.'

With regard to this we asked whether this means that if a victim can forgive then the perpetrator was transformed prior to this? To which we were given to understand that this kind of process does not happen as a general rule, but that it is a possibility, if there is reciprocation. If victims can forgive, they can do so for various reasons, perhaps a karmic one, e.g. a connection in a past life between the victim and the perpetrator. It can also be due to the influence of angels to which the person has opened himself, or the possibility can be there because of the soul maturity of the victimized human being. We should realize, however, that it is very difficult for Christ to descend into the evil of the perpetrator, just as difficult as it was for him 2000 years ago to descend as a God into earth life and into human death.

On the following day, after I had pondered all this, further questions occurred to me, and we continued the conversation. It is not the case that the Christ descends on principle into everyone who is evil. It is not predetermined that he can transform into good the evil in everybody. The transformation of death into resurrection was an act of grace for all people, because human beings had entered into the sphere of death through the Fall, without any prior knowledge of what sin and death were. This experience did not exist as yet in Paradise. Nowadays every human being knows evil in all its many guises. The transformation of evil can no longer be purely an act of grace on the part of Christ, but human beings themselves have to contribute so that it can happen. And there are hindrances put in Christ's way by human beings themselves, and which for the time being he cannot surmount. In the same concentration camp there were evil people in whom he could dig out the soul pearl, and there were others in whose case he could not do so. Hitler and others like him are irredeemable for present spiritual vision, unreachable in fact.

There is still an infinite amount of evil in the world. But it was in the middle of the twentieth century, in those twelve years of National Socialism in Germany, and in the seventy years of Bolshevism in Russia with the horrors of the work camps and death camps, that this descent of Christ into evil occurred and the beginning of the transformation into a higher good. And just as Christ's deed of resurrection 2000 years ago works further in humankind because human beings can fill themselves with this power, and with Christ within them can awaken to new life all the death and dying which they already suffer in life, just as they can experience a resurrection of their dead power of love, dead hope, their dead plans for life, likewise in every human being who opens himself or herself to this new Christ power, Christ's power to transform evil will find its continuation. And this often happens precisely when we ourselves feel weak in regard to our humanity. Paul expressed this in the words: 'For God is mighty in the weak.'

An old priest recounted that after the war he had been made a prisoner in Yugoslavia where he was put through terrible torture to force him to make a particular false statement. There came a point when he could not hold out against it any more, grew weak and confessed to the falsehood. The feelings of disgrace he subsequently felt, the feelings of guilt, were as awful as the torture. But then the thought came to him that the time would come when his torturers would have to endure an infinitely more terrible agony. And he prayed for them. That was the godly strength in his weakness. That was the ongoing effect of the new Christ deed in an individual human being.

After 11 September 2001

The catastrophe in Manhattan is the consequence of the way human beings have behaved. What led to it is the power held by a few people over everyone else in the world of finance and economics, the world power of politics. These power-mongers have been active not only in America but all the world over. The angels did not intend the World Trade Centre to be destroyed. The cause is in the human realm. What matters now is how human beings react to it. The angels showed Agnes pictures of the present moment from their point of view:

'When the twin towers went up in flames cracks went out from there over the whole earth, but these were invisible to physical eyes. From the inside of the earth a kind of gas is rising up which can be both beneficial as well as poisonous, all according to which human beings inhale it. This "air-gas" (gas-like air) makes people nervous, dazed, hesitant. It has the effect on people of enabling them to hear the voices of angels better. Yet human beings are afraid. They ought to prick up their ears.

'This was an attack on the very symbols of capitalism. The world is indignant. It was high time, however, that the basic tenets of materialism were shaken to the core. Rudolf Steiner told people that materialism is an illness. This act of terror is meant to make human beings reflect, become more conscious. This is part of the therapy for this illness. The great spiritual entity Michael wants to speed up the change in our thinking. The values of the new generation should not be those of the present rulers. After this catastrophe it is possible that progress might be achieved. This action was not instigated by the higher powers, but the time was ripe for something to happen, and it *had* to happen. That "gas-like air", which can make people ill, can also bring benefit.

Illness or health can arise from it depending on the condition of the human embryos it enters. The striving for
security, which politicians are so concerned about, is a
striving to restore old times. They want people to be able to
coddle themselves in security again. But all this is only to
placate fear and not to see the dark side of events. They
want to ensure that something like this does not happen
again. This is how the politicians react. The reaction, however, should be quite different. A new criterion for judging
such events ought to be found. But people are now in a
hurry to cover up these cracks so that they cannot be seen
any more. But they are there neverthelesss, and this rapid
covering up makes no difference where the appearance of
the "gas-like air" is concerned.'

Some of my readers may think they have already looked
at things in this way themselves. They may also think in this
way with regard to some of the other angel messages.
Indeed, if we look at life without prejudice a lot of what we
think ourselves is the same as what Agnes is shown by the
angels or clearly experiences herself. We can take this as a
confirmation of our own thoughts. The angels put it like
this: When people think actively everything they receive by
way of intuition comes, just as Agnes' messages do, from
the angels. The difference is that Agnes is able *consciously* to
experience and perceive the angels as beings with whom
she converses and who have knowledge of these things.

Cooperation between human beings and angels

This book is an endeavour to help human beings develop a
growing awareness of the constant presence of angels, in
such a way that this becomes an experience and not merely
a thought. The angels move through our present world, but

whether they can actually play an active part here depends on whether we give them leave to do so, whether we open ourselves to them. After the Concorde crash in July 2000 an ecumenical memorial service was held at the exhibition centre in Hanover. The Catholic bishop, standing before the mourning congregation, cried out: 'Where were you, God, when the accident happened? Have you forsaken us human beings?' And the Protestant bishop asked: 'Why did this have to happen? Why did God permit it? I do not know.' Where catastrophes are concerned God is held responsible and not humankind, yet human beings do not let God into their researching, their inventions, their actions and their thinking. The messengers of God, the angels, need the collaboration of human beings who turn to the angel world so that they may enlighten our thoughts, enabling us to see from a higher vantage point what needs doing; and so that they may awaken our hearts, enabling us to become aware that the One we love lives just as much in every other human being as in ourselves, because he is the true human being in every weak earthly human being. For instance, particular qualities in another person can make us suffer. But then we notice that these are the same qualities we ourselves suffer from. If we now add to this the thought that the true human being, Christ, suffers these to the same extent both in us and in the other person, it can move us to the point where love will awaken for the One who himself suffers both in us and in the other person and yet—or just because of this—does not forsake us. And it is the same thing with regard to the joy we feel about the stages of genuine transformation taking place both in ourselves and in the other. Here too, we find Christ as the One who rejoices with us. And it is through experiences such as this that the angels find access into our lives.

The purpose of this book is to help promote this

cooperation between human beings and angels by impart-
ing the angels' view of the great problems in today's world.
It lies within the freedom of every individual person
whether, and in what way, they want to cooperate. May
each one of us respect the freedom of another person who
does so in a different way from us. This book, too, the same
as its predecessor, was written out of a voluntary wish to
follow the advice of the angels.

Irene Johanson

What the Angels Need to Tell Us Now

Receiving, Considering and Acting on their Messages

The first part of this unique book focuses on Irene Johanson's experiences of being attentive to angelic guidance during her many years' work as a priest. The second part consists of messages and information received through a friend, Agnes, who represents a new kind of clairvoyance. Agnes's ability to communicate spiritually with the angelic world has the character of clarity and wakefulness. Unlike many mediumistic or channelling methods, hers does not entail a dimming of consciousness.

The messages Agnes receives contain important guidance from the angels to humanity, including advice on how to relate to angels and how to receive clear messages from them. The book also includes answers to esoteric questions asked by Irene Johanson about the Archangel Michael, the Apocalypse, Jesus Christ, the Mother of God, and much more.

144pp; 21.5 × 13.5 cm; paperback; £9.95; ISBN: 1 902636 30 9